CRISIS: COLLECTION OF 101 POEMS

Inspired by Real Life Interactions with a Trained Crisis Counselor

Kyleen Elizabeth Oldham MA

ISBN: 9798301991639
Imprint: Independently published

This book is in memory of my dear cousin Chris who took his own life in May 2019. He was like a brother to me growing up and was always protective and gregarious. He was passionate about skateboarding and tried to teach me when we were young. He was such a bright soul who brought so much activism through his community with his thrift store business. I lost touch with him in my latter years and truly regret not knowing him more personally as young adults. He was truly a brilliant soul full of love that struggled with a broken heart and negative intrusive thoughts which he usually kept bottled-up inside. This book is in memory of the beautiful "brother" I still hold dear in my heart. I know he is at peace with his mom, aunt, uncles, and grandparents by his side in whatever life holds in store for us after this crazy earthly roller coaster ride.

Table of Contents

Lovesick - 9
Solace of My Intolerability - 11
Homecoming - 13
Idolize - 15
Teenage Angst - 17
When “It” Comes Knocking - 19
Protest - 21
Fault Lines - 23
Anxious Hourglass - 26
New Girl in Town - 29
Torn - 31
To Hang -33
Spots - 35
What I Am - 37
Worthless - 39
Shy - 41
Relapse - 43
Let Me Talk - 45
Concealed - 48
Ooops - 50
Grieving You - 52
My Nightly Call - 54
Zip Code 777** - 57
Ripple - 59
Ex-Friend - 61
Aloha Alana - 63
Gaslit - 66
Shoot Away - 68
Mommy Dearest - 70
Threats - 72
Sodium Nitrate - 74
Fallen - 77
Reality - 79
Preparation for Alice - 81
I Have Friends… - 83
Receding Within Myself - 85
Cover Me - 87
They Say - 89
Picture - 91
Fearful - 93
Overwhelmed - 95
IDK - 97
Freefall - 99
Life’s Counterpart - 101
Run Away - 104
Mother’s Touch - 106
Bang - 108
Worthy - 110
Tonight - 112
Unclean - 114
Wishful Thinking - 116
Cope - 118

Home - 120
Toady - 122
You - 124
Lost Bug - 126
How to Survive - 128
Extremes - 130
Mind Games - 132
Paranoid - 134
Biologic Dreaming - 137
Nothing Human Left - 139
Accidental Angel - 141
Fate - 143
The Burden - 145
Unwell - 147
Running from Innocence Lost - 149
Alone Again - 151
Attached - 153
Love You - 155
Reminiscent - 157
Unexpected - 160
Feed Me - 162
Left Behind - 164
Worthless - 166
Lovesick - 168
Spiraling Down - 171
Happy You - 174
Lullaby - 176
Nervous - 178
Spectrum - 180
Home - 182
Isolate - 185
Confidence - 187
Truth Hurts - 189
Shade - 191
Mama - 193
Failure - 195
Rope - 197
Overseas - 199
Overdose - 201
Daddy's Home - 203
Hopeless - 205
Overloaded - 207
Fly Away - 209
Draining - 211
Catching Flight - 213
The Cycle - 215
Ground - 217
Am I Worthy? - 219
Locked Away - 221

Crisis: Collection of 101 Poems is written by a professional Crisis Counselor with a Master's degree in Trauma and Crisis Care from Liberty University. These stories were all inspired by real life encounters where all personal or verifiable information has been removed or changed to ensure anonymity and ensure HIPPA is not violated. The poems are inspired by these personal encounters the author had experienced in her career in person and through suicide and crisis hotlines and is enhanced by pieces of original artwork displaying the humanity and raw emotions felt in each crisis situation depicted. This beautiful representation of those at the most vulnerable moments of their lives allows the reader to realize that we all struggle with mental health and it can show itself in many different forms. A crisis is not solely limited to a state of suicidality, and the author portrays the diversity of experiences and real life inspired circumstances that are stumbled upon daily in the work of a Crisis Counselor.

ACKNOWLEDGMENTS

If you are in need of immediate support and are in a crisis, please reach out to anyone dear or dial/text 988 or text "Home" to 741741 and speak to a trained crisis counselor there to offer support and a listening ear. You never have to be alone.

A Crisis Counselor will be with you shortly…

Lovesick

I keep an uncomfortable complacency,
While pacifying life's Irony with Tonic and Gin.
I gifted her my heart in a pocket watch.
She scoffed the love wrapped with time,
Tossing it under the clutter of her cosmetic bag.

Never able to satisfy her engrained preconceptions.
Endless insults sprinkled salt on my ruptured chest.
The deep sting in my gaping wound gave me purpose.
As she griped nonsensical insecurities till I cradled regret.

She sewed lace around the borders of our rubbish life.
The red lines on my raw wrists ach with toxicity.
An unquenched thirst kept our relationship moribund,
As I desperately drank the dew off the buckle of her shoe.

Caught in her spider web to then realize,

I was only tangled in the twine I ensued.

Solace of My Intolerability

On the precipice of this finite line,
No sooner to the fall than a fly,
But with the anxiety of an inexperienced orator.
Thoughts grasping at the atomic particles,
For a sense of grounding and security,
When all else feels terribly displaced.
Despair is my only brother in arms,
In the front line of this subsistence war.
However; this bloodshed has been depleted,
Leaving only an illusion and fallacy to coddle my wounds.
I have known no other role to play,
In the rapture of self-inflicted incapacitation.
My mind is only an enigma of laceration.
Ceaseless tapping within my skull,
Unwavering towards any provoked aid,
Only contorting the dismal dissolution deeper,
Into my versatile vein.
Always ushering me back to the finite line,
Of the ineluctable precipice of my conjecture.

Homecoming

He is my solemn disturbance,
The quake beneath my feet.
He is my home.
I beg for a scrap of consideration.
He would rather instigate through disregard.
The apprehension nauseates me.
These thoughts tunnel burrows through my cerebellum,
Prompting reminders of his deceitful escapades.
Secret infatuations grew into sexual explications,
To recant the vows he had undertaken.
He affirmed to never deceive me again,
Or maim my ruptured atrium.

My sister refused to forgive his lack of conviction.
She would bolster me when my body betrayed me.
Her strength gave rise to my wilted wings.
I never got the chance to fly.
My sister is now enfolded in the earth.
The essence of my support eternally nullified.
I am left to perpetually slip in his excreted venom.
His cunning words dilute the poison's acridity.
I linger with his guile amongst vexing insecurities.

I garden in stagnation meditating on what's obsolete.
The upturned soil harbors this metallic odor of defeat.
It reminds me of her youthful laughter.
She would come to the porch and holler,
"It's time to come home for supper."
I darted to her with the swing still swaying,
I heard the metal chains rattling and colliding.
Now I turn and I see him in solidarity behind me.
My swing is motionless as he will seal his grip,
On the chains that once supported me.

Idolize

I crash against waves of white powder.
I am wrapped in a snowy bedspread,
But my mind won't permit me to slumber.
Nothing new,
Only recently amended.
Searching for Jubilation in hopes of deviation.
There is an end.
My mind responds with razor precision,
To slice deep into my mortal ego,
But shreds the essence of my identity.
Only desolate pains remain.
An empty shell of an anthropoid,
And dire shrieks of faded apparitions,
Tempt my tears to water the ground,
So that I can be planted beneath.
I pray for an early frost to permeate my soil.
Anything to bring back the taste of the sweet snow,
Draining down my sinus cavities.
I am gifted the illusion of life while blighted.
Upon attaining my Jubilee,
I receive the deceptive snowy embrace,
Perpetuating a warmth that is not material,
But solely the shooting of neuronal duplicity.
Before I can realize the ploy,
I am already six feet below.

Teenage Angst

I am screaming,
Beneath my porcelain shell.
Why don't you see me?

Standing in my long sleeves,
In the dead of summer.
Do you know you will bury me,
With your lack of empathy?

I cannot hold on much longer.
What is there to hold out for?

When the one who gave you life,
Refuses to presently spare it,
It all feels so hopeless.

Simple affection derived from an embrace,
Saying, "It's going to be okay, I am here for you",
Can be enough to evade my entombment,
For just one more mere moment.
But you refuse,
As you just play along with the porcelain.
Does it make you feel more comfortable?

Sorry that I am such a burden to you.

When "It" Comes Knocking

Titter-tattle, Prittle-Prattle,
A Teasing tickle within the fissures of my mind.
Fittle-Fattle, Dittle-Dattle,
Electricity shoots within my arterial walls.

Thud!
The cement pours over my chest cavity,
Shhhhhhh!
It hardens with haste,
Compounding the inequity of my regrets.
Ik-ik-ik-ik-ik-ik-ik,
Flutters against the walls of my coronary valves.

Swoooosh!
The gut punching exasperation,
Ignites the conundrum of my inhalations.
Hawh, hawh, hawh, hawh,
My breath grapples with my lungs capacity.
Zzzzzzzzzzzzzah,
The pain threads through the gyri,
Of my ever darting mind.

Ziiiiiiip!
I slide within the walls of my own flesh,
And begin rocking with spontaneity,
Seasoned with layers of cumbersome tears.
No sense of time,
Never ending.

Protest

I don't need the persistent chatter,
Clamoring down my left ear canal.
The noise unwaveringly traverses,
Across the intracranial air,
To only exit from its brother on the right.
Nothing retained.

The boundary is already in place.
Yet, you remain standing in your high-waisted jeans.
The bridge of your specks,
Kissing the blush on the tip of your nose,
Flushed from distress.
Your distorted conjectures hold no weight,
But your Coke bottle glasses,
Offer no chance for understanding.

Insight is inapplicable as irrationality protests.
Even if I scream, "This was never about you!",
Your ego will not allow the truth.
My candor cries that I need my space.
I crave the time of solidarity,
Within the confines of my bedroom walls.
My growth demands an accommodation of privacy.

Your attachment and insecurity,
Will not allow any empathy.
The selfish means of your coddling.
The only child of a single mother,
Demands of you a need of codependency.
I seek individuality,
Postulating a sense of independence.
Relinquishing the tethers of my childhood.
Please, let me be…
Free.

Fault Lines

It will NOT work.
I have tried before.
Already have done that.
That has NEVER helped.
It is NOT enough for me.
That is NOT how my brain works.
I canNOT stand the idea of that.
NOTHING can distract these thoughts.
I have always felt this way,
And I guess I always will.
This NEVER helps.
My brain is built differently.
I have NO one.
I am always a burden.
I do NOT want anyone's empathy.
I do NOT deserve it.
NO one understands.
I can NOT get better.
I am NOT worth your effort.
Sorry to waste your time.
This has only made me realize,
How my only cure is my demise.
I do NOT know.
I can NOT tell you.
You can NOT fix me.
Been there and done that.
Everyone is annoyed by my presence.
My family does NOT understand.
I do NOT talk to anyone.
I have NO interests or hobbies.
There is NO way to be motivated.
I do NOT know why I am even still here.
There is NOTHING I want to do anymore.
It only hurts to exist.
I should have left years ago.
Everyone will be happier when I am gone.
NO one will even miss me.
NO one will ever notice.
I will NOT burden them any longer.
I am only ever a disruption to their day.
I will NOT make myself their responsibility.
They are tired of the stress I create.
They could NEVER accept me.
All I do is console everyone else.
NO one ever asks how I am doing.

I can NOT say that I will be safe.
You can NOT do anything to assist me.
There is NO point in trying.
There is NO improving.
Life is all just a joke.
You are only here for the money.
…
Are you still there?
…
Hello?
…
Help me…

Anxious Hourglass

He is new.

Peering and fixated,
Attempt to lock eyes.
I gaze upon my boots,
As I navigate to my work station.

He is new.

A steaming tea kettle whenever I walk by,
With an unwavering ego.
I pull my chin to my chest,
And fixate on the tile,
Dodging cracks in the floor.

He is new.

I falter as you approach,
Grinding the rubber of my heels.
I breathe deep to swell my lungs.
I assert my boundaries,
In crystalline fashion,
To mask my anxiousness with assertiveness.

He is new.

Distant whispers of my name sprinkle every corner,
Till I find my way to his car,
Perplexed and disoriented,
With a lone water bottle of unknown origin,
Seal broken and half drank without context,
Secured within my clenched fist.

He is new.

Lightening shoots down my spine.
Radiating flames while I am fixated frozen.
My voice submits to the petrified silence,
As thoughts formulate behind mute lips.
Scavenging for a crumb of remorse,
Amongst an army of men in hard hats.
Feeling dazed from the secular cycle,
In the dark concave of my mind's walls.

He is new.

The steel toe of my boot,
Lets me kick the brick foundation,
Which harbors my impending panic attack.

He is new.

I sit within the confines of an armed oak chair.
Sweet cinnamon favors the air.
Behind a desk her eyes spoke,
This deep harbor of infinite empathy,
Without uttering a single phoneme.

He was new

I close my eyes and take a pause,
Placing two fingers on my wrist,
Pressing into the vein to ensure I am alive,
As the pulsation grounds me in my seat.
I take a deep breath before I speak,
"I need your help because of him."

HUMAN
RESOURCE

New Girl in Town

A barrier to stave off two siblings,
From provoking the apex "big brother" duo.
A hurdle marked with acetone and face cream,
Buried beneath miles of lashes,
Kissed by scents of amber and sage.

Classic bully syndrome with a fake tan.
Pushed away from my own sense of security.
Falling down the well of delusional wishes,
Never perceiving any change from loose change.
Marinating in abandonment and trust issues.
Contemplating the definition of "family".

Sibling rivalry.

Once amicable with a bond like epoxy resin,
Now control emanating through coral lipstick,
Simmers ceaselessly as background noise,
Preventing fraternal transparency,
Deserting all empathy.

Running into the backyard hyperventilating,
Burying myself within the trees and weeds,
To only be greeted by conceited cops,
Perpetuating a rouse of compassion,
For an annual salary and residual pension.

Returning home with wagging fingers,
Left in a room that was not mine.
Mourning my parents,
Alone.

Torn

We stampede down school halls locking arms.
A companion I should trust with a life.
My undying paranoia crawls like microscopic mites,
Generating an insatiable itch across the brain.
Trust broken by the hands of another,
Spawning a distorted perception of humanity.
Sporting bloody hands from the abuse of loved ones,
Through the placing under contention of their compassion.
Littered with parasitic excrement of lies and deceit.
To feel betrayed by my own thoughts,
While simultaneously unable to harness back control.
Fawning unworthy in the relationships I seek.
Incapacitated by my personal disparagement.
My insistent self-loathing igniting the doubt within,
Ultimately pushing away those who love me.
To leave me ruminating in my own self-destruction.
Haunted by the trauma of human duplicity,
Unable to fully exterminate every lingering egg,
Ensuring a perpetual cycle of intrusive self-deprecation.

To Hang

Just a thought.

A single thought cannot hurt me.
I don't have the rope secured yet.
But I do have a necktie of my father's.

Just a thought.

I need the bar in the closet to support my weight,
So I can extinguish the smoke in the mirrors of my mind.
They creep like walking shadows in each ripple of my brain.
The deafening screams overpower any reasoning.
I need to take a step of faith and kick the chair from underneath me.
Praying the primal drive within me to preserve the life I have left is silent.
I feel with my bad luck that my body would ultimately betray me.

Just a thought.

Doctors have pushed two decades of pills that only flatten me.
Crippled motivation lingers with the accessory of a bitter aftertaste.
Unfit to curb my degree of instability and dejection towards existence.

Those are just thoughts.

Similar to the orchestrated serenade of oxygen deprivation,
Resulting from the heavy bass of carotid arterial compression.
My skin turning a flush plum as my consciousness slips.

Just a Thought.

Or with my luck I will live forever brain damaged and catatonic,
Forever alive and eternally entertained with just these thoughts.

Spots

My heart weaves infinite bruises,
Saturating my body black and blue.
Black and Blue.
The same colors of the police sent to my home.
My last crisis conversation escalated to trauma,
As I only wanted support to prevent an attempt.
Cops dragged me through my door,
Before a counselor would even listen.

Black and Blue.

I know my address populates your screen,
Littering personal information to use against me.
I am pathetic enough to render unto Ceaser.
That is why I cannot voice the urge to cut with this razor.
You must believe that I am safe hearing the words I say.

I am encased in Black and Blue.

I have isolated to sulk in the grief of the schism within my relationship.
Imprinted with his abhorred disdain that emitted from his chestnut eyes.
Fixated glare like my mother's when I unintentionally break her china.
No remorse in the coldness of her dishware love affair gone awry.
Even in her hospice hospital bed she would never say "I love you, Julia".

Black and Blue.

Never mind.
This resource is useless.
I think I would rather die,
Than speak with you again.

Just a morbid Joke, of course.
Goodnight.

What I am

Ripped off the wall.
Torn into shreds.
Scraps crumpled in a tight ball.
Submerged till soaking wet.
Disintegrated in the water.
Decomposed to a puddle of mush.
Penetrated by my fingertips.
Smeared in disarray.
Coated the mahogany surface.
Dried into patchy blotches.
Adhered like Psoriasis.

I glare upon the wreckage composed.
Removing my pocket knife in preparation.
Unfolding I begin to peck at the wounds.
The patches progressively hardened to concrete.
Each chip from the blade flaking off insecurities.
Scrapping trenches releasing powdered anxieties.
Attempting to crack through the complex disparities.

Once every last fiber of paper is out of sight,
Only scars remain etched in the wooden finishing.
Some grooves running deeper than mendable.
The table's original appearance long forgotten.
I scavenge for paint to mask my ingrained distrust.
Choosing to be forever alone.

Worthless

Contraction of romance through a siren song.
The wafting melodies are alluring in the distance.
Each chord wrapping me around each measure.
Drawn towards the heart of the scaling octave.
The enchantment's gravitational force pulling me,
Each note's sweet taste then rapidly turned to brine,
As I was dragged under by a merciless riptide.

I am what lies underneath the dark waters.
Stretchmarks, blemishes, moles, scars…
Failure, guilt, desperation, isolation, emptiness…
Released from the psych ward on Tuesday.
Craving unconditional endearment and adoration.
Harnessing affection through consistent desperation.
Blinded by conception of an eternal twin flame,
Until he kicks me out of his black Ford F150.
Left on the side of Lincoln Highway at 3 in the morning.

Raindrops soak boulders into my clothes,
Imprisoning me in my shame 7 miles from home.
I sacrificed my body for a prepossessing hymn,
Sold deceit packaged as respect and devotion.
I dropped my boundaries three hospital stays ago.

Fallen and trembling on asphalt,
Drenched in the stones thrown upon me from the Heavens.
Flashed by a phone notification for another profile match.
Tempted to once again swipe right even with God's detest.

Mom assured me this utter disease of eternal emptiness,
Secured by her love of dope ensuing my abandonment.
I am a shell of a human that can never be satiated,
Always chasing Prince Charming in a cycle of exploitation.
Delusional sense of validation forever gifted in false idols,
Alerting me from my inbox as the perfect match unveiled.

Shy

It's me.
I take the blame.
Scapegoat complex.
Trembling at my sinews.

My family is an institution,
Of mentally deranged requests,
Planted by my mother's regrets.
Formulated by broken generations.

Litany of insecurities crafting chaos on the family tree.

Thrusted into the role of my mother's caretaker.
Demonstrating a betrayal to my illusion of stability.
Now in constant position to honor the lunacy,
That dementia adds to the already sick mentality.
I have no honor as I currently hold one foot in the grave.
Regulating daily through chronic pain and personal disability.
Mother stretches my rubber till the point of popping,
Filling me with her ignorant fibs to rationalize her neglect,
Then forgetting my name when I need to process childhood reflections.

Rang my sister to prune the disparities from my limbs.
Pouring inner thoughts through unmixed paints,
Converging on canvas in abstract shapes in hues of a bruise.
While cobwebs built up in corners expanding in a mesh,
Lit simply by an apparition of moonlit fog in the distance.
Sent a photo through text that procured an audible smile.
She fawned over the beauty in each sweeping brush stroke.
I gifted my art in a means of garnering empathy and compassion,
From a sister that was raised to only gaslight and falsify.
A worthy sanction to uncover the smile lost in my eyes.

I traveled to surprise her with a visit when fall turned to winter
The picture had already been sold for a desperate fix.
Self-medicating to tame the voices and delusions,
As scripts of Haldol sat coated in dust and intimidation.
The concept of not recovering is the embalming of what is familiar.
Familiar is safe in the way we already know what to expect.
It is the canvas beneath my brush holding my deepest vulnerabilities.
Now perched above a stranger's mantle who doesn't even know my face.

Relapse

I'm going to self-harm tonight.
Relapse renegade to the blade.
The avalanche is foreboding,
Always in my peripheral view.
Work, School, Black Student Union,
"Yes", "Sure", "Okay", "I'll try",
Surplus of hopeful fallacies,
Titrating failure and self-loathing.
Nil offered as recompense.
Slaughtered and then scolded for my lethargy.
Irony leaving one catatonic.
Glassy eyes, wide, contrived self-destruction.
Irreparable as it is incomprehensible,
To subject anyone to the answer of "no".
Immediate combustion of any relationship,
Smoldering scraps of reparations and embers.
Thus, the Eroding walls of my proclivity,
Remain fearful of wavering.
Fear of rejection, resentment, detestation…
Thus continued proliferation of solicitations.
Break me down.
Breakdown.
Avalanche.
Flooding thoughts of worthlessness,
Drowning in insecurities.
Hollow.
Vulnerable.

How many pills must I swallow for this all to go away by tomorrow?

Let Me Talk

I broke my covenant with God.
I relapsed on dope.
The National Security Agency,
Spies on me through my phone.
I may seem insignificant,
But phones are so easy to hack.
How could they resist?
The Government doesn't intervene.
It would expose the full scale,
Of our surveillance state we ascribe to.
And they broke into my home,
Destroyed my security cameras.
I summoned the demon Leviathan.
The Gematria of Leviathan is 828.
I was born on August 28th.
I am the antichrist.
Syd died,
They say she was just surveillance.
She loved me without judgment.
Meth addicted and intelligent.
I tried to help her to get clean,
Ended up using dope so she wouldn't leave me.
The Psychiatric hospital said I have schizophrenia.
It is just another way to discredit me.
No diagnostic test is needed,
I know the paraphilia that I am stricken with.
I only look up drawings.
I do know how to get real images.
I have a level of restraint.
They started monitoring me to access my pixels.
Traversed motel to motel to evade.
One day I went into a rage.
I blamed Syd for everything,
But she was the only one that understood me.
Syd was on my side the whole time.
Syd didn't die.
She is in witness protection.
They think I am some criminal mastermind.
I delete everything off my phone.
They judge me even off the small portion,
Of the dark parts I house,

Just like everyone else.
The one friend I have validates me,
Through homelessness, losing my job, being stabbed.
I tried to convince my counselor Syd was still alive.
My sisters' altercation ended up with a knife in my lung.
A fight over my drug addiction,
Ended with me on the brink of death.
I said DNR,
They still saved my life.
Now I have to make a decision,
As they are probably going to hold me for medical detention.
I am stuck between waiting for the swat team,
Suicide by cop,
Or taking my own life.
There is no rehabilitation.
It simply pushes me to the outskirts of society.
Debt, foreclosed home, repossessed car…
Mom doesn't deserve another child that is a felon.
They changed my phone password,
So I had to wipe it clean.
They have all my pixels,
But I am not the mastermind they seek.
My friend wouldn't bring me alcohol.
It would have made this easier,
When I pulled the trigger.
I've wanted to kill myself since my 20's,
Scars running up and down my forearms.
If my paraphilia became public knowledge,
My mother would be forced to ostracize me.
And maybe I am evil,
But I have to make a decision.
I live on the line between life and death.
A swat team is coming to raid me.
Can't trust the government with their current genocide.
Authoritarian and observing quietly,
With their silent all-seeing eye.
I must leave.
There is no time for goodbyes.
I know they are reading every word I transcribe.
Please let my story be known,
How the NSA has treated me.
I leave my judgment to God now.
Goodbye.

Concealed

To deflect my thoughts from my team's utter defeat,

I tumble into the confines of female fashion design.
A craving felt down to the calcium in my bones,
As an impartial means to manifest my feminine energy.

Questioning the extent a make-up brush can reconstruct,
Or the victory to be found in a blouse, heels, and bangles.
Pondering the illusionary effect of long full brunette locks,
Or the swift scent of citrus and rose eloping the nostrils.

I have attempted personal make-up conceptions,
Adorning varied hues against my cheek bones,
Emanating a sense of raw confidence.

Man or woman; masculine or feminine.
Forever dissecting ceaseless fashion trends,
To adapt a means of fitting my contour.
Rummaging seasonal pallets for complimentary shades,
While anxious at the uncertainty of my own acceptance.

A litany of unwavering thoughts put up barricades.
Pondering if my parents could still love me.
Forever entombed in isolated disparities,
Those racing insecurities.
A ceaseless appetite like nicotine,
Constantly seeking.
Vibrating at each hair follicle,
Unable to leave my skin behind.
Stripping my ability to shift my focus,
From everything that I can never be.

I really thought my team would win tonight.

Oops

Heedlessness wrapped in laziness,
Adorned with an apathetic bow.

The bottle said two… I took four.

I sat ignorant till my stomach gurgled acid,
Water flushing out of me,
Restlessness questioning mania.
Legs elevated as my head swarmed,
Aching in the anxiety I created,
Praying literacy to be my savior,
As I peered through the needle thin lettering,
Spotlighting my impetuousness.

Worrisome nightmares plague my sanity.
Reminiscing prior lethargies,
A provision to my eulogy,
Proclamation by lunacy,
Casted in an effigy of foolishness.

As the Reaper feeds from my fallacy,
I am mindful of my biology,
Fantasizing my liver malfunctioning,
Till all is inoperable and I am left lying,
My consciousness ceaselessly reflecting,
On the number that transitioned me,
From symptoms being alleviated,
To a sudden ambush of terminal panic,
And ultimately an untimely demise.

I only needed two… but I took four.

Grieving You

Walk away…

Won't look over your shoulder.
No second thought.
An acquired sense of contentment,
In turning your back,
Organizing priorities.
Transcend from what once was "Us".
Reopen the wound you say is healed,
As you pull the threads of stitches,
Through my epidermis.
You demand to cut all ties,
To remove your own sense of guilt.

I drip in woe.

Friends tap your crystal while chipping my china.
Reminded that Isolation remediates my disfiguration.
Penetrated arteries enamored with martinis.
Bar hopping as she studies Pilates and real estate,
Riveting spirit of a job coach and exotic dancer.
Perpetuated an entanglement,
Desiring a fling,
Deserting my sentiment,
Towards a perceived mutual infatuation.
Implying a shroud of duplicity,
To which I am lying on a bed,
Cheeks consistently hydrated for three months.
Left as a shut-in with swollen tear ducts,
Caked in the ash of an undying cigarette to ease my woes.

Your face forever buried,
In the synapses of my mind.

My Nightly Call

Foreclosed by the medical system,
That cannot stomach to foot a bill.
No scraps of dignity left behind to feast.
Precarious ticking impending obliteration.

First neglected for my spinal fracture.
Exposition on the x-ray was dismissed.
The medical system handed me muscle relaxers.
My body is still seizing from their indifference.

Tonight,
No amount of threats could secure my safety.
The guns already taken into possession,
By the officers that have lost their trust in me.
Days have passed and he grieves,
Holding the ammo of his weapons,
Like the sentiments from the bereaved.
They stole his right in a plea for my well-being.
Such an unnecessary violation to seek.
I was left culpable from my own mental instability.
Soon even he will leave me.

The situational satire is laid in the facts,
I have five more ways to kill myself forthwith.
Through my grinding teeth it is my declaration,
They have chosen for me to die tonight as their gift.

The senseless ego from a man in uniform,
A catalyst of relentless welfare checks with guns drawn.
Violated physically through the legality of a badge.
Slipping GHB discreetly into any lipstick stained glass.

Go ahead and send the police,
Have them draw their weapons at my door.
I pray to be gunned down,
To have the raging tornado in my mind nullified.
The spiraling desolation of this mental storm,
Surging at a velocity of dissociation no more.

The Sheriff's Emergency Risk Protection Order,
Snuffed out the rights to my own life.
So with this object in my hand,
I will end it all tonight.

No lawyer can defend my destiny of self-destruction.
Each day I still lay a garden lily on my father's grave,
Finding solace in the comfort of seeing him soon.
I am broken,
A defect,
Failed by the system that created me.

I must hang-up,
My children want to play on the tire swings.

Zip Code 777**

Marinating in my own self-discrepancies,
I tap acrylics against my keys.
Beauty creates a barrier for productivity.
It is hard to see realistically when lacquered,
Seven coats deep.

God questions if I am part of his creation.
He should know by my genetic mutations,
Proliferating markers of instability.
It is a title I commenced with fallacy,
From a lineage mapped by the divine hand God heeds.

I'm sorry.

These qubits run a two-track system,
Yet the complexities of my functionality,
Puts me back in the dark bind,
With an eyebrow shaping razor,
Against the forearm of the perspicacity of time.

The stress is inebriating,
Beyond what any recreational high can enhance.
The antidepressants first offered sustenance,
Then stripped the brace that reinforced my stance.
I stood at the edge next to shreds,
Of what once was a precautionary line.
I pieced tatters into braided chains,
Creating an illusionary cohesion of my mind,
From chaos and unbridled pain from the divine.

Ripple

Normalcy of the mundane work day,
Interjected with an incident so divine,
Triggering an anxiety that was so familiar,
That danced with childhood trauma.
A pirouette of tainted beauty.

Her toes tip the first domino stacked.
Tumbling dominos tickled the floor's surface,
Trailing off into a ceaseless void.
Expanding its black hole to swallow me.

Complex is what the Therapist deemed me.

Failed part of a system that never wanted me.
Harassed for my ethnicity, gender, and disability.
The utter torment of this formulated enigma,
Left a list of chronic denial in my back pocket.

Two managers claim to defend my reputability.
This gave a sense of foreign and benign security.
File folders labeled with monograms heightening my blood pressure.
Nervousness penetrating the oak of an antique desk,
Lingering with the scent of a springtime pumpkin spice.

Her pinstripe pants suit was paid by a six figure salary.
I recede within myself,
Knowing she cares more about her company.
Far more than a multidimensional minority,
Rippling a sea of bubbles claiming victimization,
By a fellow manager's pale white hand of superiority.
He keeps his team together with an ego that binds,
Escalating the prevalent inferiority that is thrashed upon me as mine.

Noticing her tightly pulled bun placed high on her head,
Highlighted her inability to see my value through her entitlement.
I sit as a simple disabled female Navajo American.
I can stand tall even with the degenerative disks in my spine,
I have not lost my sense of ancestral pride,
Even if my employment ostracized me to my tribe.

Ex-Friend

Diagnosis: Schizophrenia.
I was not aware of the incessant fallacies.
The pills barely curbed her delusional reality.
Heels dug in the dirt as an anchor of stubbornness.
She rejected any alteration beyond her comfortability.
Comfort is not always what is healthy.
Comfort is only known and routine normalcy.
Every bath was beyond reasoning.
I stood with kakis and a blouse each morning,
Assisted her with her daily life functioning.

Facts were fleeting as we tripped down rabbit holes.
I couldn't keep up with the altering yarns she spun.
Each chalky pill was more sedating,
Her apathy wasting her motivation,
The physical stupor left in dirt and rot,
Her mind would run a marathon unwavering.
Paranoia rattling in the tail end spiral,
Of a full blown air show collision.
I am the only spectator to marvel.

Bloated barbaric caricatures fancy her mind,
Of the family that yearns to only support her.
She would lie to the world as I spoon fed her sustenance,
And proclaim a sense of stability as a cure,
As I extract heaps of hoarded rubbish into half ton bins.
Her bites leave you with the anticipation of venom,
But only yield scarification and a broken home within.

Last autumn her son began to mirror her symptoms.
She shoved him in the back closet to incur a similar fate.
Complaining residual loneliness as she brought me in her home.
One moment she would label me divine and then charge me with my crimes.
Not once could she hold a conversation with her own flesh and blood.
He disappeared to get high after a scrimmage with mom one night.

I am gracious to have known her,
But I don't know her anymore.
She mitigates when I walk out the door,
When our friendship will sever ties.
But her lips can't muster the words,
To accept the truth of my fading shadow,
Knowing she will again traverse alone,
Through the terrain of a disillusioned mind.

Aloha Alana

Nice to meet you.
I do appreciate you.
My mind is molting,
Leaving me naked.
Exposed to the frostbite,
My skin is cracked blue.
Susceptibility to intrusive images,
Leading to rumination of my sins so lush.
Deciphering what caused him to withdraw from me,
I find myself with the blunt end of a plastic brush.
I begin to beat myself in punishment and rage,
Falling to the floor defeated as panic engulfs me.
Half a bottle of Benadryl in my hand is calling my name.
Flushing down the pink capsules with saliva I placate.
Gazing at the bottle with an orange label reading "lethal".
There was no respect for its contents with my disparity.
I pull down my comforter as a burial shroud ritualistically.

I awake eight hours later in a ghastly state,
As an extension cord is draped around my larynx.
Flashing images of talking to the nurse at discharge,
She asked, "Why reach out for help if you don't want to change?"
My thoughts scream,
"Should I just jump off the seaside bridge again to please you?"
"Is this the support you offer me?"
She must have see n through my feathers as I was molting.
She knew my true worth,
All I wanted to do was fly forth.
I went back home to the friend whose car I stole,
For a joyride to the bridge to set me in flight.
Suddenly realized her son was in the backseat,
Eyes drip trails of the Nile River in his car seat.
Parked seaside to drop him with grandma.
Left a note in his book bag asking for empathy and a pardon.
I darted to the bridge and released myself into the sea.

He was the only one allowing me to release my demons,
That have isolated me in the shade of my cognition.
Perpetuating an ideology that my identity was priceless,
To ultimately walk away deserting the fledgling he caressed.
Molting till deteriorated and scavenging for relief,
From the crumbs of pain life had fed me.

With no intent of finding a way to remedy,
Beyond the bottle of pills for my fabricated allergies.

And nothing you say can ease my mentality,
As I strive to reach a sense of vitality,
By the hands of my own reality,
With one foot in the grave.
And you are not any different,
Than those who hath forsaken me.
I am ready to end the chat.
Goodnight, my lovely.

Benadryl

Gaslit

Lack the ability to participate in the expectations of reality.
The overstimulation suffocates my sensory perception.
Crippled to the floor with my stomach twisted in hitch knots.
My temples throb with thought of social engagement.
My spectrum has me detained and bound at the extremities.
It strips my humanity with its illusive decree of absurdities.
The eccentric enigma threads like an intricate spider's web.
I become a caricature to mask the disability entangling me.
Mother clears the cob webs which fractures my placidity.
She refuses to acknowledge my falter from a functional human being.
And the web with my name is crushed between blades of the broom's straw.
Now she rewrites the son that fits her needs and satisfies her complacency.
I am left with passive aggressive conjecture as I relentlessly weave,
Striving to break from her standards and garner neuro-divergent favoring.
Mom sweeps me back to the floor in a search for manifested fantasy.
Inhibited and drained within this cycle of an unappreciated child of diversity.

Shoot Away

I fantasize about shooting up my school.
Rejection and ostracization is purely cruel.
I ask not to be accepted anymore.
I have found my calling through true crime's door.
Serial killers to mass shooters seeking notoriety,
Through inflicting pain to display their personal deity,
A God that seeks fair retribution for one's agony.
A bully gets met with a bullet of equality.

I may not seem like a martyr to the naked eye,
Yet my sacrifice will be glorified by those under similar strife.
In no light would I go unnoticed to the world surrounding,
The first time my presence is taken with accountability.
Disrespected boundaries that pierce the flesh,
No longer forebode a dismal prey but allow full relinquishment.

Crashing waves of epiphany to the actions carried,
Without time to repent before the punctured cry.
Fearless against the impending authorities,
Surrounding as my dopamine floats exorbitantly.
Pondering my fate before the tide retreats beneath me.
Yet I reassure this is only fallacy as finally I am free.

As the daydreaming reverberates against my skull.
Isolated at my desk buried in my hood and headphones,
Blacking out the tribulations of my present circumstances,
Lulling in the comfort of my own visionary narrative,
I conjure the fragility of the mental construct of home,
And ponder at what moment of my titration,
I was rendered to ascend alone.

MAAGUMS

Mommy Dearest

Reverberating nervous proclivities,
My body has no means of compensating,
As my heart accelerates contemplating.
Mom meditates in her recliner.

The air breathed in intolerable silence.
I need the morphine to kick in,
To get me through the repeat clinical revelation.

She is stronger than I,
She is undeserving,
Of her body nursing her deplorably.
Doctors deciphering crumbs of abnormality,
Of a mass of pure perplexity,
As this enigma refuses to wane,
And only adapting to multiplicity.

My stomach crawls up my throat,
My head cycling ceaselessly without answer.
Mom sits blunted and in a void,
My perturbation swelling,
Creeping through every pore of my body.

Mom dozes next to the lamp,
Illuminating a dull cast in the den.
I can't entice her to sleep in bed.
She can't accept such comfort amidst uncertainty.
I toss back sedatives to inebriate me further,
An escape from her turbulent reality.

Threats

It is simply an impending truth.
Waiting for the follow-through.
Each call reaches automation.
No living voice of confirmation.
I hesitate to call authorities,
When my paranoia may not align,
With the reality at play before me.

Dubious uncertainty in your words,
Uttered under your breath at this late hour.
I cannot refrain from the electricity,
Radiating a sense of panic within me,
That screams of your demise,
Without need for any validating

Attempt to determine my level of interference,
As you tried to lull me to sleep,
Assuring me everything would be fine,
Before dropping connection on the line.
You are the one who wants to die.

The fractured sense of sensibility,
Is nothing but a tremor beneath me.
To call police could risk our rapport,
Fracturing our relationship at its core.

I could lose you in any context:
Alive, dead or pending in purgatory.
Restlessly anticipating some finality,
To allow me to breathe in your name again.
There is ceaseless anticipation in my heart,
A sense of quietude lingering between friends.

Sodium Nitrate

At dawn I press my lips against the bag,
A ritual executed each day I rise,
Since its arrival in its brown packaging,
Taped and shipped with no ill intent.
It is my savior in white crystalline form.

I have attempted with bleach and ammonia,
Only for my fragile body to seize from its toxicity,
Knocking over three buckets of chemicals surrounding me,
That were once perched in a triangulation.

Shipped to a facility in frictional socks.
I took a chair into the bathroom between nursing rounds.
Secured a towel around my neck, draped it over the door.
The chair I stood on was the only barrier to my relief.
I slid the chair aside with my foot so softly.
My pelvis jerked as my peripheral vision faded black.
The force of my weight slid my head loose from my noose,
Leaving me half dazed on the slick tile floor,
Counting the dust balls from stray hairs and lent,
Until nursing made rounds again.

I was fed into longer programs to ease my adamancy.
Each felt like a step backwards with new epiphanies.
Most notable was the day with outpatient telehealth therapy.
My mind's shell cracked,
Ooze spilled that yoked with my lack of sexuality.
It soaked through each gyri and sulci,
Images of molestation and abuse from elementary.
Inflicted upon me by an older cousin's hand,
Who restrained me to submission and silenced me with threats.
Then my computer screen turned black.
I was left to fester in the infestation of my great awakening.

Week's isolation led me to binge my prescriptions.
I felt ashamed to speak on my incestualized exploitation.
Awoke in ill-fitted paper garbs and wrist restraints.
Doped on Gaba with no recollection of my resistance,
As medical staff swooped to rescue,
My enthusiasm to their attempt was lacking.
Found mixed with medicinally induced psychosis,
Made white walls an unwelcoming familiarity.

Determined myself to be discharged into the arms of an escort,
Sought to overcome my sexual hesitancy and heal my ineptitude.
It was a grave mistake to trust in my unstable mentality.
As I left the motel with whispers of my name from every stranger.
Possessed in the silhouette of my repeat victimization.
The voices pressed phone screens to faces assuring me I was recorded.
Now pornography spread rampant of my naked vulnerabilities.
I was the fool who brought on my own indignities.
Trusting a whore with her intentions set only for the dollar tucked in her breast.

Lost the loyalty of my job to new management's tyranny,
As I was dismissed for not respecting their company's rubbish heap.
Left to rebuild a sense of myself on a third shift schedule,
Till the Sodium Nitrate arrived in its paper parcel.
At the top of my shift I bid this earth a fourth farewell,
Exhausted and entitled to the relief I seek.
Shaking away the paranoia that is riddled through me.
For the Sodium Nitrate to finally fulfill me.

Fallen

Began with losing my livelihood,
Igniting the embers of my failure.
It became sobbing wretchedly on your shoulder.
My plunders lessened into simple blunders.
There was no judgment in your embrace.
That was yesterday.

Tonight.
I sat rocking restlessly in grandma's cradle.
Antique pine wood was refinished in her memory.
Swinging as you enter in a fit of militancy.
I can't refrain from calling your name,
Smote in my vibrato as I anxiously plead,
"What is creating this hostility in your tenacity?"
You plunge past me,
Thrusting yourself forward,
Till you hound belligerently to leave you alone,
Isolating within the walls of our bedroom.

I break.
The panic pulsates to rhythmic drumming,
Leaving me to question my own accountability,
In the emotions you were dispensing.
Frantic thoughts of leaping off the third floor balcony.
Impulsive need to cut sense into my epidermis,
Easing emotional intensity with physical fracturing.

You then return somber requesting my empathy.
My purpose is redefined in your complicit eyes.
I'm safe.

Reality

Nothing is real,
When living in an imitation,
Stripping away any sense of purpose.
Some would consider this fanciful.
It is merely a struggle with no prospect.
Death is simply to slumber with no awakening.
The world is like a cardboard cutout,
Or a set for a stage play,
Putting on the illusion of something complex,
But viewed at the wrong angle it is seen for its defects.

Nothing even matters.

I struggle to hold on.
Consistency is only found in my suicidal ideations.
Life is simply a chaotic love affair.
Drops of antifreeze in my morning cup of coffee.
Collectively it will soon consume me.
Now I unnoticeably sip the toxicity,
As my lover sees me off to the factory.
Labor that feels mechanical in my tendons,
As each fiber of my muscle recedes.
It is as if my body is not engaged in any absolute.
I am lost in a dream consumed by mold.
I am the decay infested with rot,
As life's decoy is made of plastic.
My mind fixated on this single thing,
"I should fall asleep and never awake".

Preparation for Alice

Anna would tell Sarah and Nicole, “You never cared, so fuck off”.
She would tell Austin, “Look what you did! That should be you, not her.”
Mom and Dad would mull amongst the putrid bacterium of my decomposition.
They will ask themselves, “Why didn’t we call more? We could have stopped her.”
Sam would spiral, but my note would console her,
As I will tell her that my cat Leo is her responsibility to care for.
Jonah will be eager to get a fix for his morbid curiosity,
By writing my eulogy and speaking before the sanctuary’s pulpit.
The sacramental nature of my body in the refuge of steel and zinc,
Resting on a cloud of white silk and down feathers,
Placed before an assembly of long-lost relatives and family members.
Dan will make my funeral service mixtape.
Cousin Sam will get the best lighting as he captures my gothic portrait,
Photo of caked on macabre with adhesive, cotton, and eye caps.
None of this keeps Cousin Sam from posting it for his social media content.
Aunt Janet will sit in the back with 6-month old Piper lulled to rest.
She keeps diapers at hand in case she needs to change her in haste.
Piper is swaddled with her blue bonnet nestled deep in her dreams.
She has not the faintest idea of the lingering corpse in the vicinity.
Auntie Alice now is a distant memory lost in her underdeveloped neural circuitry.

MIX
CD

I Have Friends…

My continuity does not always add up.
Sunday, I am singing Sondheim in a red tutu,
Clicking heels on a glossy stage floor.
Huddling in our thespian tribe with arms enveloping.
Threading through curtains in the wings.
Stripping attire to slide on a new character's skin,
While peers slather me with make-up,
Placing bows in my wavy auburn wig.
Gripping interlocked fingers with a squeeze,
As we curtsy and bow to our patrons and spectators.
Quivering with adrenaline, dopamine, and sweat.
Gossiping about our success and the thrill of an after party.
Eager to share in the reflective treasure of our experience.
Heading to an exclusively reserved restaurant to carouse.

Then I didn't show.

Not a single vibration or subsequent notification.
Complete ostracization and lack of appreciation.
No one, nothing, emptiness, isolation, contemplation,
Caught in an isolating cyclone of intrusive diffident cognitions,
Ingraining my barcode against the algorithm set in place.
This only depletes the DNA that defined my identity.
Deserting the faceless shell of a once bustling beauty.
Slipped through cracks in the clan's foundation,
Tossing aside my credibility to a cast of my craft.
Relinquishing any genuine concern for my spirit.
I am an apparition against the backdrop of an absent epilogue.

Receding Within Myself

Just got out.
Mom lashes out at me like a troubled teen.
Tug my sleeves past my knuckles and am buried into my hood.
Her words still pierce through like a viper's sting.
Belittled as I recede in the shell of a helpless toddler.
Rattling how I draped her with stress like Christmas garland.
Bickering of adapting home for my safety,
When impulsivity and self-loathing is suffocating.
Excessive guilt to flood my arteries,
Throbbing veins at the seams of toxicity.
Mom displaced frustration for hostility towards my infirmity.
Keeping my vitality hostage to her insufferable nagging.
I am always the excuse for her indisposition,
Not the liquor and noxious relationships.
She mapped me a guide to inpatient hospitalization,
Through an ex who demanded I kept cutting,
Conniving Mom through his flirtation with control.
He left Mom who defended his contention to be needed,
To bite the neck of his new vulnerable victim.
I am now the reason of his abandonment,
Released to an empty room encapsulated with denunciation.
I crave the bare stone walls and weighted doors behind lock and key,
While remembering how I never truly had a "home" to simply be.

Cover me

Displaced at only fifteen,
Lacking sentiments of family,
As my capillaries blacken the bruising.
My body caved away from any touch,
Due to ingrained preprogramming,
From whoopings to unwanted caressing,
Commencing before I consciously recall.
I concealed marks with clothes and creams,
Scared of the unknown instilled by intimidation.
The fruit of my flesh I cannot expose,
With no trust left within my sternum.
No crisis team or authorities have believed me.
I only ask for a civilian of the same fruit,
To be sent down MLK Boulevard,
Towing a blanket to cover my vulnerable pulp,
And warm my blemished skin,
To only leave me once again,
Alone on the streets I will call “home”.

They Say

They gloated about the anonymous letter.
The gossip carried like a molasses river.
Indulged in a spread of sweet and bitter.
Passed ear to ear under my nose,
Till my olfactory system exposed,
The rumored betrayal of my own lover,
In the arms of a divorced coworker.

Confrontation yielded an excuse of “work related”,
Till inquired about the floating notation,
Rich in a plague of speculation.
He hysterically denounced an affair.
Headstrong he would proclaim:
Counseling, church, communication, and prayer.
A genuine lover in desperation from guilt or contempt,
As a small town rallies around a note and stamp.

Ink bled no compromise in the town’s eyes.
Friends threaten retreat by severing ties,
If I refuse to comply to leave my relationship behind.

Trust stripped like bark to reveal the termite infestation,
Wavering my structural integrity through fake relations.
Proliferating weakness as I am chewed raw and regurgitated.
Nothing to support me when I snap under this declivity.
So my timber plummets in isolation,
Leaving me with spikes of anxiety and hastening rot.
I lay stunted in reproach of my own lack of final decree,
Leaving me diligently crushing apple seeds with my molars,
From the decaying fruit I had procured in this atrocity.
Continuously consuming till there is no more feeling.

Picture

He threatened to transpose my formal guise to pornography.
The photos of my face to be planted onto lude female bodies.
False depictions then propagated digitally to his pervert buddies.
A victim in some pedophilic scheme to decimate my aspiration.
A humiliation that would bar me from a law degree at thirty.
Any speck of respect swept under the rug of disillusion.
Left damned to poverty and an abusive relationship.
Forced to further degrade myself with sexual exchanges,
A transaction where he slips his body in for my financial gain.
Accumulating in homelessness and addiction from broken sanctity.

I am just fourteen.

Sought friendship through a forum craving to vent bottled emotions.
Was met with sarcasm about teenage angst with sexting slipped in.
Far from submitting for the compromise of companionship,
I inevitably refused complicity and set my moral boundary.

Thrusted into an infinite oblivion of quasi-particles and black matter,
His attempt of black mail left me floating deprived of oxygen.
Collapsing through the asteroid belt leaving me with abrasions.
Tossing me inevitably through Saturn's rings that sliced my skin.
Fearing the plummet back to the dooming gravity that crushes me,
Like a vulnerable speck of dust left in a state of numb isolation.

Shattered before the computer screen,
Tears flood into a pool at my feet,
As I pray to be electrocuted,
So no one will know how I failed.
Liquefied in his lies that have forever damned me.

Fearful

I'm okay…but,
She told me that she relapsed tonight.
Cross-stitched her arm with crimson "X"'s.
Her family belittled her artwork,
It was only "attention seeking",
It was not from the heart.
She was deemed an impressionable copycat.
They labeled her a disappointment to their ancestry,
Ridiculed for being an imitation of their bloodline.

She is currently on the other line.
Trust for adults dissipated into fog.
Age does not connote maturity.
Her tears are a fierce hissing sea breeze.
Stubborn as the dock amongst the irrational waters.
Scoping for a ship that never comes to shore.
Hypnotized by the sea line against sunsets.

I am a fly caught in her crafted tapestry,
Enmeshed in the threads of her artistry.
A web trapped in my systemic tree,
Powerless to see the ground from the leaves.
My prowess weaving beneath my wings,
Prowled upon by the kin that begotten her.

I feebly tap at these illuminated keys,
"Can someone help her, please?"

Overwhelmed

Never knew the limits to my capacity,
Till I had already burst at the seams.
Spewing gasses mixed to toxicity,
A conundrum how they never killed me.

Ruminating in the possibility of my insipid thoughts,
Of dying at the hands of armed robbers,
Veering through the guardrail on Deal's Gap,
Or being left in the street gutter for a dollar.

Self-loathing has stained my skin green,
My gaze moving from the barista throthing lattes,
To the homeless man reading his newspaper bedsheet.
I have wasted my life with such tenacity.

There is not an ounce of freedom to entertain.
My father took his problems out on me,
My mother coddled me,
Leaving no room for autonomy.
Lost in a labyrinth of malignant tumors,
Needing to cut away these learned behaviors.

Thoughts and feelings that are theirs and not my own.
It has left me in eternal expansion of phantasm.
I fled across the ocean to face my reconstruction,
Which instead was evaded by video games systems.

I continued to run but never escaped.
Compulsion for Intimacy splintered my nerve endings.
I disengaged my power source,
Removing any motivation within me.
Rejection became my familiar face.
Even the one woman who allured me,
Could not tote all my excess insecurities.

The product of two ruptured hearts of abusive lineage.
There was never an ounce of hope in my veins,
Just toxic fumes pressing against seams,
Till I too ruptured,
Leaving only the skin of a man behind,
As the boy continues to run for his life.

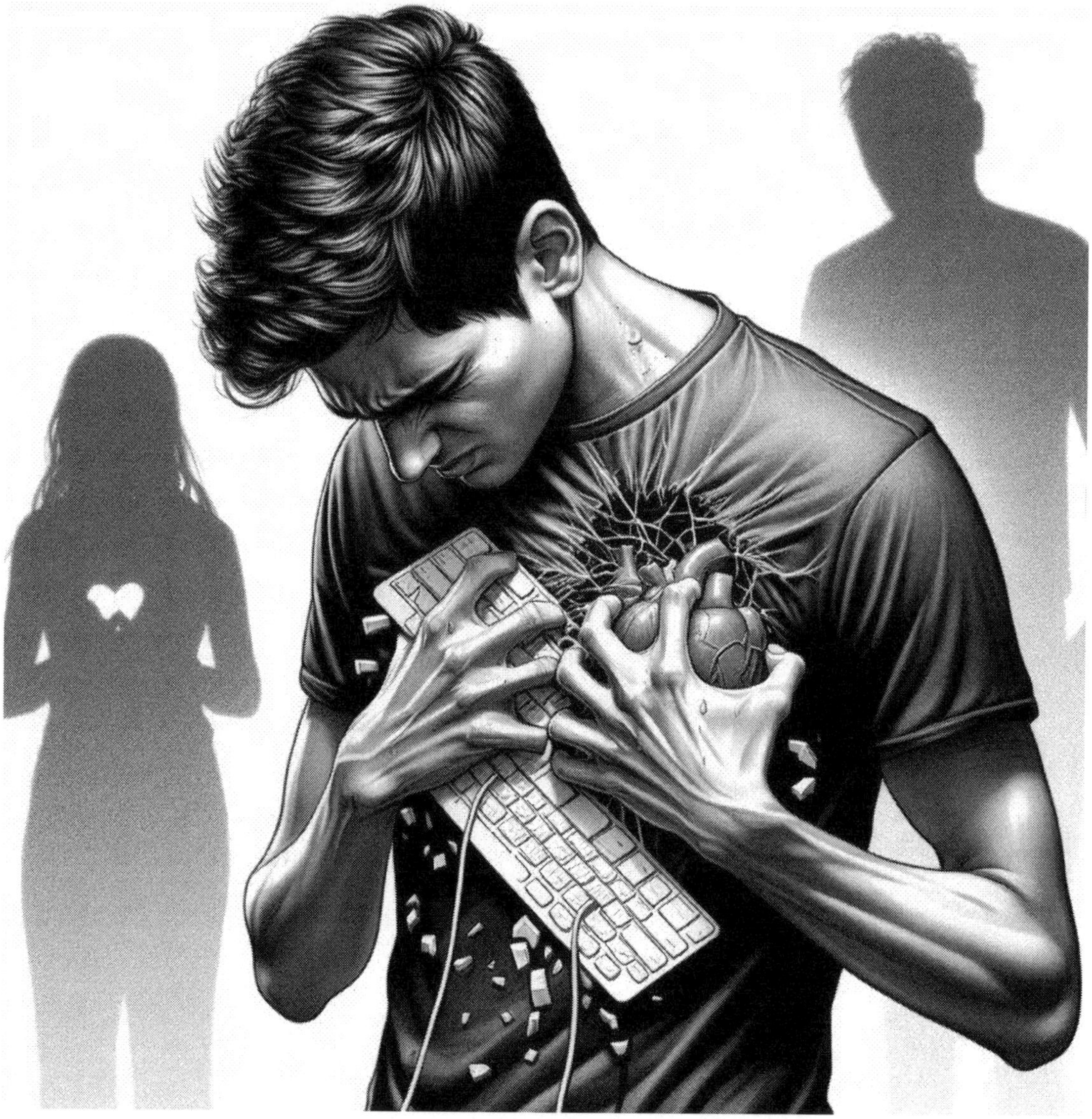

IDK

An utter sense of raw hopelessness,
The foundation of my marriage has slipped.
The communication is null and void of emotion.
Every utterance twisted into an argument.
Combativeness that yields only a dagger,
Piercing the aluminum armor I adorn.
I once drowned in my own spirits.
Her grudge is etched in stone,
From the residual trauma I composed.
Always unintentional in its repose,
Poured out only when the booze hits my gullet.

A sustained pain unyielding from her memory.
Her heart was scarred past rehabilitating.
Six months sober for the pleasure of the flies.
My wife sees nothing but the abuser in my eyes.

If only I could use a syringe to drain,
The incessant booze lingering in my veins.
My arterial walls corroded with its poison lining,
Tarnishing any chance for mutual solidarity defining.

Now my sobriety is a prison of my feelings,
Fermenting in the transference of my wife's agony,
That I solely created out of my own addictive tendencies,
Layered in my weak sense of morality.

No amount of being clean can regress,
The injury marked by the keloid scars on her chest.

Freefall

Depleted balloon floating to the earth that it once levitated from.
Once free on an exhilarating whirlwind adventure.
Unable to even catch its breath before another gust blew by,
Sending it traversing farther and higher into the unknown void of sky.
Illuminating curiosity off its thin rubber shield,
Feeling so invincible yet authentically fragile.

Suddenly the convergence of wind from north and south,
Caught the balloon in the middle of its spiraling collision.
Visions of a thimble trigger traumas of the needle.
The deafening "pop" feels all too real in the uncontrollable corkscrew.
Ruminating on the helium that birthed its plump taunt form,
A sense of resonation passes with the temperature deviations.

Taking for granted fortuity and contingency,
Only highlights deficiency and negligence.
Motivation is waning as rubber begins to contract.
The agile dance transpired into a pitiful descent of despondence.

The illusion of vulnerability propels a sharper decline.
Through a relapse triggered by trauma from flashbacks created by spontaneity.
All that remains is the wrinkles in the rubber.
Strikes familiarity to winding scars,
Perpetually displaying the image of feebleness and uncertainty.
Ultimately all that is left is toxic habits and a sense of abandonment.

The shriveled rubber balloon drapes over the tree branch,
Of the towering oak tree with the wooden swing,
Outside of that house I grew up in.

Life's Counterpart

I didn't ask to be raped.
The liquor took effect so quickly.
First night, first party, first drink, first lie.
Mom thought it was a slumber party.
The college crowd was intimidating.
Fourteen never felt so juvenile.

Then he came along and soothed me.
I trusted a jester who spewed lies like jokes.
My trust slipped under his sleeve and he pulled out flowers.
When he leaned in for a kiss his make-up smeared.
I pulled away and he poured me one more shot.

The waves that transpired through my body,
Drifted me off to sea.
I felt too heavy to fight the current.
Then the night swept in with a heavy fog.
My sight became limited.
I numbed myself in the cold waters.
His touch was ice.
Then the fog began to wane.
My body was still caught up in the riptides.

He pulled me out of the sea into the back of his Sedan.
My breath became short-winded as my pruned fingers dried.
Images of Mom danced in my head as I yearned for Innocence.
Suddenly an open door left me to a tumbled lump of dry debris.
Washed up sea algae and sediment serving no purpose.
Five miles away from home on the side of the road.

The Sedan only a distant memory once my vision sharpened.
Slumped in discomfort as the dissociative breeze lifted me.
Traversing with the images of Mom dancing in my head.
I withered in the knowledge that I had lost my innocence.

Home.

Lectured for trying to swim underage.
Mom was unknowing of how far I had already drowned.

Now it's week three of being restricted to my deserted island.

Water still floods my lungs as I look at the plus sign.
This was the third attempt removing any room to deny.
There was an infestation tearing me apart inside.
This fin rot only reinforced the futility of my terminality.
I went into the bathroom to let the water begin to flow,
Yearning to be carried back out to sea.
A bottle of diphenhydramine as the current sweeps me away.
No one will have to be exposed to my blood-sucking pathogens.
We will let the tide take us away far from shore.
I know they will forgive us,
Me and the parasitic child I now adorned.

Run Away

I just wanted to talk to someone before I died.
The chalky pills left a sour taste in my mouth.
I could not flee the flashing images behind my corneas.
These embedded memories are branded deep.
They fed off misfiring neurons that taint my unconscious.
It would prove quite lethal to cut out this disease.

I fail to muster the will to utter their names.
The darkness that stole all comfort amongst their shadows.
Daunting words tease the prospect of recovery.
Though my job was left behind,
The trauma still hides.
Crippled to the box spring as gravity suffocates me.

All this access pressure demands I alter my matter.
As my bones scream for the ease of this painful compression,
I stomach bottles of tiny pearl shaped candies to ease my strife.
With each swallow I prayed it is enough for my transformation tonight.
No need to call *911* and burden those I labored for.
I hindered them enough when I divorced from the police force.

I appreciate you listening.
I simply craved a compassionate ear.
Now I shall drift off to sleep as my eyes are weighted.
Your time was much appreciated.

CONGRATS, NEW IN THE FORCE

Mother's Touch

The caustic nature of the thick wool fibers,
Coated in keratin,
Is what bound me to you.
It was now time to sever the tether that lingered.
Never yielding to my sense of complacency.
Freedom was designed to inhabit mistakes.
You were never fond of the craft.
You saw no skill,
Only a premeditated blunder.
I could not tell you how I was nauseated from the normalcy.
Everything has been so constrained and routine since Dad's passing.

You were manic at the beach video chatting with old high school friends.
You are forty-two.
The embarrassment bled outside the lines,
Diluting the once vivid colors.
Your proprietary blend of instability, uncertainty, fear, and grief,
All gift-wrapped and adorned with the bow of the mask you wore.
Never being able to escape the dead,
Adapting to complacency to numb the pain.

The pain never goes away.

Contemplating if the ground you perch will offer adequate support.
Ruminating on the empty time you will have to fill this void.
That abyss where intrusive voices snatch up opportunity.
You fail to rival their assertions,
Slipping on the mud beneath.
Panic begins to spiral as you frantically try to keep steady ground.
If only you would challenge those voices,
Isolate irrationalities with insipid questioning.
I observe you grasp onto cosmetics to procure the mask you honed,
Attempting to evade the exposure of a delicate canvas,
Painted by your tears and flared rosacea.
This constant concealment crossed with insufferable vulnerability,
Coddling a sense of passiveness layered in proclivity.

I knew I had to flee,
Before the tide swept me off my feet.
Only Dad could provide us with that sense of stability.
I pray you too can embrace the severance and find your own tranquility.
But I got to go.
I love you, Mom.
I will not be home.

Bang

Abruptly witnessed my grandmother pass to sepsis.
Poisoned from the negligence of caregivers.
Family flaunting egos to the desolate nurses.
Ostracized and exploited for their passive behavior.
Singling out the family members that can't say "no",
To place blame on someone in that lackadaisical home,
To satisfy the rift in their ancestral lineage,
As the foundation continued to crumble with each breath given.

Left to sit with the freshly canned raspberry jams.
Musing on the passing of my own father.
He was my best friend and card game confidant,
The support that laid my current of worries to rested waters.

Now I am tarnished and peeling up the walls,
Stripping the dingy wallpaper that lingered behind.
Walls that shriek as they chastise me in solidarity.
Flashes of Dad home alone the day of the burglary.
One lone shot to the chest,
Obliterating the heart that aligned with my own.
A rib fracture firing splitters through his chest cavity.
Splinters that I still cannot dig out from under my skin's depravity.

I fell into the arms of my grandmother,
Who the very next year was infected from being sick of me.
Leaving me with just my thoughts of this curse I have become.
And I have the 9 mm loaded in the glove compartment of his truck.
I must fulfill this trinity to prevent another fatality.
I always yearned to find purpose with my martyr mentality.
That peaceful sense of justification,
As I pull the trigger to find my way back with my family.

Worthy

If I O.D. on this medication,
Would I be worthy enough to matter in your eyes?
What would it take to eradicate this pestilential penance?
This medication lustfully invites me with its siren call.
Yearning to simply clear my head of these unfiltered thoughts.
It all began in 2022 when I was hit head-on,
Stripped of bark and left to rot with the fungus proliferating.

The medical system has surrendered me,
To manage my own aching afflictions in solitary restraint.
Deserted to smolder in the blaze of the sun,
As I pray the mirage transforms into a tangible remedy.

My husband cares.
He is the caretaker to the T.B.I. plaguing my prosaic living.
The diluted subservience shamefully labels me a burden.
My disfiguration draws downcast eyes from those I love.
I am purely a repellent without medical intervention.
A grisly byproduct of another's audacious vehicular conduct,
That had forsaken the perpetrators to face oblivion,
Consequent to the lack of seat belts or airbags deployed within.

I was their miracle clinging to life amongst the wreckage.
Subsequently I have conceived that the real miracle was six-feet under me.

Tonight

I hurt myself Tuesday.
Delicately applying pressure against the sharp steel,
Swiping back and forth like a pendulum traversing down my forearm.

I have an urge.
I attempt to pick at the skin of an orange to suffice.
This is not a preventative as it only delays.
My mindset remains fixated on self-mutilating.
My manicure carves rivers that snake across the rind.
Being 19 at this moment feels like do or die.
One single moment could steal the vast possibility before me.
My sight rendered useless through the setting of the dense haze.

Unmotivated.
I must cut out the malignancy.
My thumbs press till I bust capillaries.

Bruised.
Mom ensures I yearn to have not been conceived.
Each utterance rolling off my tongue is cultivated into an opposition.
Reluctant to even say “I love you” to only repent in hindsight of disbelief.

Alone.
Lamenting the hours spent sedentary in the closet,
Not discerning my normalcy was simply exploitation,
As Mom left for parties in hiked up skirts and ballet flats.
The circumscribed walls hugged me till she arrived back.

Unclean

I need to scour away the trauma,
Off the surface of my epidermis,
Till I am exposed red and raw.
Bathing in bleach religiously,
Scrubbing till my knuckles crack and bleed.
Never satisfactory.

It is a cross-contaminated train wreck,
As skin cells are passed by each shared contact.
Touch DNA of the woman who abused me,
Shared by a shoe walking on the same tile before me.
Endless thoughts of chance encounters and exchanges,
An inescapable cyclical chain that leads me back to that woman.
The twisted underlying irony,
Her DNA is what comprises me.
No change of household can protect,
The biological imprisonment where I am the subject.

Crippled and fermenting in chemicals with a scouring pad.
I yearn to eradicate any fragment of you that lingers unsaid.
I changed my name, gender, hair color, and clothing.
Stopped eating to nullify one pain with another feeling.
I know my girlfriend loves me,
But she does not truly know me.
I don’t even remember who I am,
With how far away I have ran.

SKEPH

Wishful Thinking

My pain is chronic.
My job is threatened.
My wife is a relapsing alcoholic.
I cannot keep up the facade.
I am beyond middle aged.
My brain is hard to retrain.
If I cannot make my sales,
My work will drastically fade.
This technological monstrosity,
Of a world hinders the elderly.
I cannot keep up,
But bills still have to be paid.
My wife had her second rehab stay.
She has already relapsed,
On the mouthwash under the sink.
Now the liquor is flowing,
The money is only depleting.
Concept of retirement is simply fleeting.
There is never enough time to recover,
When the addict isn't ready for recovery.
Each morning my body fights me,
Keeping me from getting out of bed for days.
I must return to work after the holidays.
My body has adjusted to stagnation,
And lack of any sense of motivation.
My chronic ailments and pains negate,
Any reason to continue another endeavor.
The medical dictionary marks me competent.
Yet the retirement I had honed is dwindled forever,
On failed rehabilitation and sterilizing intestines.
And the more I ruminate on my mortgage unpaid here,
The better the pistol looks in the pocket of my recliner.

Cope

She is falling to the floor.
She rolls over onto her back.
She fumbles fingers on a blanket,
Knitted with chunky and fine yarn.
As she takes her deep breaths,
She names all of the objects colored red.
Scanning the room with precision,
She then moves onto the color green,
Then blue.

She traces the grooves in her throw.
She starts to count every thread of fringe.
She has her left hand placed on her abdomen,
Feeling her lungs inflate and deflate.
She taps each finger with her thumb.
She starts to run through her "A, B, C's",
She then recites them in reverse.
She counts in sets of three, four, and then five.
She multiplies and then divides.

She closes her eyes and pictures the beach,
That she visited before her mother died.
She feels her feet sink in the white warm sand.
She tastes the salty air on pursed lips.
She sees the umbrellas decked in Technicolor,
Beside their matching chairs dotting the coastline.
She hears a seagull call his brothers to lunch.
As her skin radiated warmth,
She prayed she would not burn.

With the tension in her chest alleviating,
Her breathing beginning to moderate,
She sits up in her bed and sighs.
She reaches out to her end table,
And shakes her pill bottle wondering,
If it was worth taking two tiny blue tablets,
To ensure she would sleep through the night.

Home

I cannot stop him.
If I try to speak up then he will hurt her.
She is all I have,
I must protect her.
Without my little sister I have no purpose.
He makes me have sex with him.
It's already Christmas Eve.
My sister sometimes lingers in fear.
I can't allow his hands on her.
I want to die but I can't because of her.
I want to seek help,
But he threatens to beat her.
I feel so hopeless and Mom is dead.
Dad had already left before birth,
So step-dad is all we have.
He needs payment for the rent,
Food, utilities, transportation, and gas.
I could leave in a year,
But then she would still be here.
We could both leave together.
But where would we go from there?
One time online I reached out for support,
And the police came by to do a welfare check.
I was frozen and parroted what step-dad said.
When they left he slapped me ear to ear.
He screamed about a paper trail.
Step-dad thrusted me to the wall,
Pinned me off the ground.
His breath had a hint of garlic and rum.
I could see her peering from the kitchen archway.
She shrunk as he dragged me away.
I was thrown into the bathtub,
My head plummeted against the tile wall.
There suddenly were stars all around me.
He threw a sheet and pillow to make it my bed.
The bathtub cradled me reminiscently,
Till the left eye had swollen shut,
And the right eyelid became heavy.
The stars greeted me in my dreams that night,
But at the same time I felt I was drowning.
I had to find the Big Dipper to guide me home.

Today

Medication reminders are just skipping tracks in my mind.
Alarms misfiring like broken neurons and charts disintegrate.
Voices dilute the necessity of the pill popping.
Filled bottles faded by my senses' over stimulation.
Weighted vibrations fracture my cranium to keep me distracted.

A wet blanket of psychosis sends shivers through my body.
I see a glisten in my eyes when the voices start talking.
Days bleed as my speech slurs to sift for replacement words.
I string together a melting pot of adlibs in attempt to be heard.
Then my own brain reverberates confusion in layers,
As these regurgitated conversations get lost in time's company endured.

Soon the minutes fold in around me and weeks fade into hours.
Chaos seeks no quick stride as my reduction in speed capsizes me.
And through the cracks in this skull that puts that void in the gaze of my eyes,
A frail case of the human I was is governed by noise outside.
I could be ten light years away but never leave the bedside before me.

Grooming falls short to the untamed nature of unaltered attire.
I started tardy in the minutes then absent in the days ahead.
And these shadows closing in around me command the static,
Like a distorted radio ceaselessly buzzing in the back of my head.
And these bugs begin festering as they crawl on each skin cell,
A sensory overdrive that ceaselessly presses my panic button, so frantic.

I pound music through earbuds that still can't suffocate the racket.
I challenge the commands with conversations that can't be sufficed.
And the scratching of my skin won't ease the insects tickling feet running rampant.
Yet as the layers of failed protection only fuel this utter hysterical commotion,
I only want to know how I can remember to take my medication tonight.

You

This distortion to my self-conception,
A selfish delusion of my own perception,
Never harmed another but my own rejection,
Until this life spawned into my belly's home.
Now this body is solely no longer my own.

To protect the life preserved within me,
I must now blind my eyes to my scale's veracity.
Each ounce attained is beyond solely my own body's.
Yet that number is still unyieldingly nauseating.

Each morning, noon, and night I only see a scowl,
In the reflection of my gaze upon the physical enormity,
Of the swelling of my whole being screaming,
As I cry out for the voices to stop demanding,
That I restrict each morsel to receded further within me,
And seek the desperate fatigue to wash over my famished being.

But I must now fill this hole I have been digging,
Arguing against the numbers that dominate my mind's capacity.
Crushing diuretics from the bloating of each drop of water I intake,
And flushing the laxatives that excrete each excess calorie.
Yet with each hormonal influx sparking acid reflux,
The proceeding feelings of purging does not go unwanted.

I am found left in tears on my bathroom floor,
Comprising of more than just the prerogatives unfulfilled,
But the mood swings of a mother feeling you kick inside me.
Unable to coo you and tell you that I am sorry for my fallacies.

With all the strength you can muster I can hear you begging,
Trying to tell me to stop neglecting myself with your love,
While I still sulk in my own toxic egocentric self-loathing.
And with each of your pleas I shake in my own grave reality,
That even that is not enough to shake my overbearing egocentricity.

Lost Bug

I never knew true sadness until he was born,
Crying for relief from this unwanted blessing as I lie on my floor.
Pondering simply pushing his stroller into an intersection,
Or leaving it on the train tracks for the next passing engine.
I would walk away knowing I could finally find peace in my bedsheets.
Sitting in silence then taking a nap until the absence was noticed.
The cops could track down the scent of the stroller,
With K-9 precision to my red panel door.
Pounding on the wood till they barged in with a warrant.
This sudden riptide would pull me under a sea of guilt and torment.
To swallow my bottle of Acetaminophen would look like an appealing adornment.

The shame of these thoughts lies in another person.
They do not come from the version of myself that I know.
It is the attachment of some sort of viral abnormality,
Clutching to the base of my amygdala,
Feeding off my emotions and implanting its own.
All these regurgitated despairing thoughts,
Relentlessly pressing on impulses to hurt my own child,
And leave me layered in despair to end the life I was bestowed.

This product of my womb is so disconnected from my vision.
I feel I live on a periphery that dissociates me from my surroundings.
My mind is simply hijacked and yields no hope of escaping.
The thoughts are slowly attaching to my heart and penetrating,
As I daydream of suffocating your malleable cranium.
No amount of liquor can drown out the relentless noise within,
Or suffice the cravings of these demonic desires I have.
I only know to punish myself through burns and cuts,
Dancing around the middle school scars I had to collect.
And as I crawl to my mother pouring out my depression,
She belittles my feelings as something every mother bears.
"This is the normalcy of new motherhood and the product of adjusting,"
Mom lectures, as she lets me have a nap to sleep off the dark foggy despair.

Cradling my repugnant creation like a true mother should have.
I am comforted knowing if I were to die my mother would love him.
This satisfies my infected mind as I am drawn closer,
To take the entire bottle of generic pain reliever.
I grasp it in my hand under my pillow as I rest,
Like a promise that soon this unsolicited pain will come to an end,
And the viral parasite I have will finally win.

How to Survive

Time falters in the eyes of trauma,
Years yield to the same sting as day one had begun.
An unwavering experience of the unconscious mind reliving.
If compassion was offered then the world would choose to forget.
Delusional ideals of headway crushed by a dense cage of affliction.
Regression was my unwanted friend in the peripheral view,
Like a foreboding apparition looming just out of direct line of sight.

My heightened sense of moral shame yields no pity.
The tenacity of man is lost within my own incapable rendering.
I honed the means to cope through blotting my mind with benzodiazepines,
As the booze alone lost its flavor when the ghosts blinded me.
That night I drove relentlessly to suffice the crushing urges,
Yet found no road to ever take me quite far away enough.

The Accident.

One haywire attempt to flee the steel bars of my mind,
Leaving me handicapped to a bed of irrational thought.
Presently I live with the apparitions eternally looming over me,
Pounding conceptions of meeting my fate through terms of their submission,
Drawing closer to the flame without the wings to fly when the heat is unbearable.
A finite line that provokes a solution to my life's state of disillusion,
As taking a step forward is simply waiting to bang my head against another wall.

Extremes

Glued to my Daddy's hip at the insufferable age of 22.
Shooting stars mock my wish for fiscal independence.
This cesspool of decay from depression's longing gaze,
Rots with the distinct stink of despair sweltering in 90 degree torridity.
Medical teams best to restrain the inhuman monstrosity,
That has become my normalcy as I fall ten feet deeper,
To ensure I can never see myself free of this lesser than dirt mentality.
Curbing misery with pills in a situational night terror defines despondency.
No diagnosis of this bipolarity is enough as I wait and pray for mania's sunrise.
Nothing can rejuvenate a corpse so putrefied and infested.
No mathematical equation can account for enough of a high,
So enduring one more night fueled by unrealistic fleeting hope,
Of that final burning meteor flashing a streak through the sky,
Breaking into particles that burn in the atmosphere of my retention,
To the Luciferin fall of my redisposition to the misery intended.
Curled like a fetus in the dark trench I have prepared,
Pondering any meaning to my plummet from heaven's abode.
My memory remains scorched by my teenage atmospheric angst,
Removing any sense of beauty behind that speck of light that peers,
Abysmally illuminating the glossy tablet on my tongue before I swallow.
The precursor to a novel undesired and unread,
I pray the sun can peek through one last time before I die,
To nullify the persuasive apathy that keeps me spiraling in time's lapsing memory.

Mind Games

She looked at me with her doe eyes.
Opened her forearms and began to cry.
I didn't know someone in real life,
Could feel such emotions inside.
I was the big brother, her protector,
Yet I had only left her to suffer,
And did not have a way to aid her.
I was useless and inferior.
Nothing would stop her.
She wouldn't tell mom,
I couldn't betray her.
But she kept finding a razor.
Even after the dozens,
I had procured from her.
Then one day there were pictures,
My best friend sent the group chat.
She opened up her forearms.
I couldn't even get to her.
She suffered a psychotic break.
They sent her off for a hospital stay.
I didn't even know where.
She could have never come back.
The anxiety I never felt before,
Swam through every nerve within me.
Then my sister got a pencil sharpener,
And tore the blade out in art class.
She came home with fresh cuts,
Under her long-sleeved hoodie.
It was the heat of midsummer.
She handed the blade secured,
Between pieces of toilet tissue,
Blotted with dried muddied crimson.
I struggle to understand.
I simply cannot stop her.
THC became my therapeutic friend,
As I tried to run from the perplexing feelings.
Now it only nullifies my agitation,
And leaves me feeling disappointed after smoking.
Without a sense of right or wrong,
Leaving me hopelessly empty and isolating.

Paranoid

They are constantly concocting a ploy.
I secured cameras around my property.
Supplied by the cost of my dead Uncle's inheritance.
The neighboring apartment keeps me awake.
I listen to the bickering and children wailing.
The dogs constantly barking, never once let outside.
There must be feces smeared up the walls.
These children hardly leave, never at school.
Endless domestic disputes across paper thin barriers,
Carries such tension that my stomach gets twisted.
They have come outside and loitered on my land.
The male has stolen my groceries that were delivered.
I have them brought to my back porch by a stranger,
As I can no longer leave my residence.
The fear that strangles me keeps me stuck in quicksand.
I peer through a window outside,
The male has gotten in his truck in the middle of the night.
He has rifles laying in the bed and one in his lap.
We make eye contact and he starts sizing up his prey.
I have no defense, a camera cannot stop a bullet.
Suddenly a shot is fired leaving a hole in my wall.
I now use this as a peep hole to be more discrete.
As I stay awake all night watching the shadows move outside.
Loitering on my property to steal in the night.
My blood boils in rage laced with terror and defeat.
Missing from my backyard shed are tools and concrete.
They must be selling them for their dope addiction.
I reached out to the landlord in desperation,
But he is part of this ploy that they have instigated.
When I inform the police and display my evidence,
A video of their domestic violence in their front yard,
They simply listen but dismiss my credibility.
The police favor the landlord who is a veteran.
Maybe they are all conspiring together to move drugs,
Through the county and state and traffic illicit substances,
Originating from across the border, arranged with the cartel.
They want everyone addicted and then profit from their suffering.
I reached out to the FBI and have not been acknowledged.
Is there anyone in the country that is not corrupted?
To partake in illegal activity and protect the criminals,
As long as they are benefiting from the profit?
I am now trapped, listening to the incessant barking,
Of three dogs whom I empathize,
As they also are unable to walk outside.

Their sharp barks pierce my heart as I hopelessly cry.
I used to be somebody, in medical school locally.
I had to drop out in my 20's due to this neighboring insanity.
It was like a light switch that pulled me into darkness.
I could have been someone if that neighbor never moved in.
How have I been placed next to such wickedness and sin?
High alert and heightened awareness,
This is my damnation.

Biologic Dreaming

I will create you in a lab with my genetic engineering.
I will multiply stem cells and even place my DNA in you.
You will be my infant, then child, but eventually my wife.
I will ensure that you have every trait she harbored inside.
You will have her strength, wisdom, cooking skills, and hair color.
You can be a fighter, but also a wife and a lover.
It will take time, but I will raise you in the way she was raised.
As you grow I will see her shine through your eyes each day.
I will dress you in her garments and take you for a ride.
We will journey off to Japan so you can see your home land.
But this will all have to come with time.
Right now I am only beginning my college education.
To receive a PHD and had access to the medical necessities,
Of a laboratory offering such opportunities to edit your genome.
For now I am daydreaming while holding my body pillows,
With the image of you printed upon them to warm me at night.
I wish that they could hug me as I wrap my arms around them.
And I have the Anime in the background playing,
I can hear your voice whisper through the speakers.
It is almost as if you are in the room by my side.
But you will never be able to just go outside with me.
You will never be able to wear your favorite sportswear,
To go for a jog in the evening when my anxiety is high.
I only jog alone and mourn the lack of your presence by my side,
As I hold the necklace like yours that's around my neck.
On our anniversary I went out to grab sushi with peers,
But nothing replaces the thought of your presence here.
So I lay back down with my daydreams, so vivid and true.
Maybe I can simply manifest you.
And I can finally have my waifu.

Nothing Human Left

I am hollow.
The shell of the human condition.
I have been gutted hollow and stranded.
There are no provisions to preserve me.
I dry and shrivel in the blazing heat.
A fragmented piece of who I used to be.
Envious of the beauty in the mirage set forth.
New state, law school, new start to life.
Refining my identity in a town that doesn't know me.
Met a boy who seemed to understand the requiem of my past blithe.
Rejuvenated in the hope of genuine acceptance afar.
He stole that from me in the back seat of his child-locked car,
Obliterating trust.
I submitted to the darkness of my room,
Comforted by the familiar voices on my television set titrating.
My body pleading for my stolen virtues to be returned.
Enunciating my speech to play victim was nauseating.
It felt easier to live as the shell that I had accrued.
What was stolen could never be reclaimed.
So I am left out in the desert to look at the mirage,
Of what my life could have ended up being.
A new start, a new career, a new refined personal homage,
Teasing my gaze in the distance as I lay withered and void in my Land of Oz.

Accidental Angel

I laid eyes upon my dead parents at only five years old.
Screeching wheels and a glass snowfall amongst twisted metal.
Mom's limbs were twisted in the wrong directions,
While Dad flew ten and two till he bent in half around a tree's bough.
He had soared ten feet through the shattered windshield.
Apparently I was the only one wearing a seatbelt.
Dad's road rash tore off most of his baby blue dress shirt.
His pants were completely stripped from his lower extremities.
Mom's body was in angles a contortionist couldn't reach.
Her hair was matted with blood that kept it stuck to her cheeks.
Medics pulled me away as I desperately clung to Mom's hand.
I didn't even get the closure of attending a funeral service.

Through pity and monetary gain, I was adopted.
The needs were met, but the parenting was repugnant.
Constant bickering echoed around corners and down the hall.
Communication only capable through loud noise and argumental downfall.
Mom's rules were unrealistic and crossed personal boundaries.
I couldn't eat without nausea or sleep without nightmares surrounding.
When I was old enough I escaped through working overtime hours.
Burn out was quietly looming as I stay away from the house of horrors.

I had picked up pebbles from the trail I made that dreadful day.
I yearned to find my way back home, where the dead could live again.
Twas only a fanciful yarn to be spun, but along the way I met her.
She found me on my trail of no finite destination.
She took my bruised hand and gently brought me to safety and security.
I no longer scratch myself raw when she is lying next to me,
No matter the burden of my parents' own insecurities upon me.
I know that I have her, my guardian angel, nonjudgmentally fawning.
Undeniable love as she insatiably comforts my broken body.
Pricelessly, I forever adore the light in her eyes calling me home.

P

Fate

They just released me.
"Discharge" is what they call it.
Let loose into the real world.
One without adult babysitting, structure, and routines.
Presently sitting in an efficiency unit awaiting placement,
A temporary holding cell till I have my adult apartment.
I long for decaffeinated coffee and Peanut Butter sandwiches.
Having snack while sitting in a circle for group,
Trading fruit cups because I liked peaches and not pears.
Having a support system of those with similar stories,
Mental health workers dotting every corner and security.
Now I sit alone in uncertainty as I don't have income financially.
I left my job four weeks ago when my mental health declined.
I remember thinking about my mother's anniversary,
Not marriage, but of the day she had passed away.
Skin pale as cotton, all the veins were profoundly blue and violet.
She didn't even know her surroundings,
She could not even utter a single word the week before.
Mom pulled out her IV and her bile drain and fell to her knees,
The nurses said it looked like she was praying.
They brought her back to bed with her knees black and blue.
She only lasted another hour before falling to the floor again.
She laid for ten minutes before staff came to resuscitate her.
When her heart began to beat, her vitals were so very weak.
She was unable to regain consciousness, slowly drifting,
Vitals falling till she was no longer breathing or her heart beating.
They did not help me in the hospital to manage this pain.
The grief still shreds my insides till I cough up blood.
And the pills look so wonderful sitting on my counter.
If I just took all of my diabetes medication,
I would get confused, lose my speech, and be too dizzy to walk.
Then I could fall to the floor praying till my heart stopped.
I just want to be with my mother again.
Being alive comes with real life stressors,
But nonetheless I still have the desire to end my life.
My community services board is helping me find a new place.
This schizoaffective disorder is crippling me each and every day.
I am worried that I will not be able to afford the bills and upkeep,
Of an apartment that is too much of a responsibility.
And mom never left me to struggle on my own till her passing.
I do not want to go back and be admitted to inpatient hospitalization.
Nothing garnered but pill bottles and a death sentence,
To escape back to Mom's embrace.

The Burden

I will not mitigate my pain by drawing others' towards my trauma,
Like a gravitational field that won't let you go without mutual transference.
It brands the back of your neck so you can be left with a scar of compassion.
While empathy drains the joy you once harbored for another to feast.
The selfish act of placing the burden of one's own strife upon an innocent bystander.

I will not provoke a parasitic mentality towards the process of my healing.
No other victims need to be procured from my inability to recover independently.
My parents are financially struggling and dealing with health complications.
It seems unfair to appear so healthy and yet approach them with such a burden.
It does no good for anyone and only initiates feelings of failure as a father or mother.
No need to waste the youth gifted with my petty inability to write off the intrusive thoughts.

It is scary how well my brain knows me to be able to manipulate me so easily.
I become one with its lies about my self-worth, hopelessness, and lack of self-preservation.
The demanding reasoning of sufficing the incessant screaming in my ear of my failures,
With the box cutter recovered from the tool box left open in the bed of my uncle's truck,
Provides a sense of personal coping and surviving in a way that suits my mentality.
Flesh means nothing when we are all only sacks of meat harboring a conscious being.

Or maybe I am simply excusing my mental instability through false rationality.
Morally, as long as I do not harm those around me with my own trauma narrative,
Then I have succeeded in meeting my personal expectations for myself.
And if I cannot find a means to manage my own mental health,
Then maybe I am not strong enough to be given the responsibility of life.
Yet, to tell anyone that would make me a hypocrite and displace my burden.
That is why I keep my goodbye letters stashed in the upper shoebox in my closet.

Unwell

Night is not my friend.
I am alone in my room again.
My thoughts are spiraling on a whim.
I lost control of my emotions.
This has been a daily ritual.
Lying in bed being self-critical.
Trying to find a reason to end it all.
This all begins at nightfall.
There is not a necessary trigger,
Except the loneliness that haunts me.
To be put through such mental rigor,
Has not helped my blind eyes to see,
Through the darkness that is before me.
Trapped in the nightly routine.
Eleven years of grueling penance,
Constantly showered in my incessant crying.
The lingering salt stings my wounds.
Never healed, only empty, numb, and drained.
I have no one to turn to pity my pain.
Sometimes I feel deserving,
I will fixate to continue to spread hate,
Upon myself and the existence I bear,
To punish myself for simply existing here.
It is perplexing when what is comfortable,
Is the fear of ever trying to become better.
So I hold hands to bind with my misery,
Blinding my eyes to the concept of “free”.

Running from Innocence Lost

My flower was plucked at the age of six.
My Mom is kind and supportive of my transition.
Vandalized by the cousin on my Step-dad's side.
My mom always uses my correct pronouns.
He was fifteen when he started touching me.
Mom even makes sure she will not use my dead name.
I told mom when I was eight what he had done to me.
Mom immediately got me a doctor's appointment for top surgery.
My Step-dad defended his nephew and blamed promiscuity in youth.
Mom was gung-ho about my FTM breast mastectomy.
Step-dad told my mother that I wanted it and now was lying.
Mom was always by my side when I came out transgender.
Mom stuck admittedly beside her new husband's side.
Mom even got my Testosterone injections filled.
Mom's marriage fell apart after another year of gullibility.
Mom got me a binder and wardrobe from her tax return.
If I try to bring the rape up, mom will defend her ex-husband.
Mom has been treating my bandages in bed as my chest heals.
Mom let that same cousin stay in our home and shared my room for two years.
Now I am coming out of top surgery while laying on bed rest.
Mom says I need to let go and move on and be a new me.
My chest is flat under these bandages like I had dreamed.
Mom struggles to even make eye contact with me.
Oddly, for some unknown reason, I still don't feel happy.

Alone Again

The room is a hive swarmed with festering bees.
Business suits bustling to lax any consorting.
A single touch radiates pulsations forever emanating.
A crescendo of noise against the ear drums feels decimating.
Voices collide in garbled speech and word dribble.
Laughter bellowing out in unprecedented intervals.

The tap drains fermented barely into glass mugs.
Conversing tables are drowned out by a distance strum.
Such music so distant is abrasive against the social conjecture.
Screens illuminate with the chaos of colors and lectures.
Iridescent signs imprinting brand marketing's disease.
Eternal dousing with alcohol and ashtrays to snuff the pleas.

Distraction arises by the brush of another against my shoulder.
A fleeting moment of mortality through human connection to another.
The beer settles in my stomach watering down my inhibitions,
As I ruminate in such a lively room of my utter isolation.
Reminded of others' joy around the restraints and chains of liquor,
I fall into the stewing of my own monotonous lack of vigor.

I pry a maze through the drowning sensation of sensory disillusion,
Raising a white flag in retreat from this social contusion.
Fleeing to the sense of solitude that wanes my chest's angina.
Returning to the empty motel room wrapping its silence like a hug.
The television is my only need to create the sense of social illusion.
I pull closed the curtains hiding the roads of claustrophobia and confusion.
It is just another lie that permeates the air of another night repeating,
Against the canvas of the bedlam of life surrounding and ever fleeting.

Attached

There is a vacancy in my heart and a void in my cranium.
Dopamine screams fulfillment through a man's affection.
Someone to stay with me more than an hour.
I want forever.
It is hard to explain.
But the chemical dependency puts my brain on the back burner.
The fireworks explode my aorta to the melody of love-bombing texts.
My chest aches to ensure no chance is missed.
Gullible to subside this neural sickness.
I slip through foolish hoops to tie off to love's illusion.
The shot radiates euphoric bliss.
The inevitable tango of kisses and cuddles while snuggled,
Slipping out of underwear and sliding into sex.
The hit of Dopa attaches me to someone I barely know.
Then to become unadded or blocked when the door is closed.

After the high I realize I need to shift my mind.
Focus on my own insecurities and lack of self-pride.
I recognize my need for others' validation and loving.
The demand of my craving is beyond troubling.
Needing a male's romantic words, touch, attention, and gaze.
A relentless desire unable to fulfilled beyond a day.
My old therapist said I have Borderline Personality Disorder.
I spend half my day on dating apps for the fix of a potential partner.
A man who holds a solid disposition and a temperament that is disciplined.
Ultimately I find myself abandoned by cheaters and fakes.
No one to take the bait of the concept of a ceaseless date.
The lost motherly affection of being coddled and cooed,
Fabricated through misconceptions transfixed on a love constantly overdue.

I met one guy a week ago.
Sensual touching ignited a spark within me.
Then NO texts and NO calls. GONE.
There is no ability to aide this relentless addiction,
Pulsating through my veins for the fix of a masculine touch.
Warm flesh feeds my cold skin as I tremble for warmth.
The marriage of bodies brings life back to my broken heart.
Only fleeting.
Soon I am ripped apart without the illusion of a text.
My brain just leaves me alone to cry.
Then the cravings reignite till they spike.
Crippling me to search for just one more night.

Leso

Love you

Keep my wings to a flutter so I am not a bother.
I cannot take flight as depression grapples me to the floorboards.
Anxiety vigorously pulsates through my hollow bones.
I can feel the animation of my nerve endings overflow.

Another altercation with my husband sent him into flight.
He packed his shiny trinkets in a suitcase tonight.
The value of our relationship left in metallic thimbles and needles.
He flew out the door with his shiny hoard of materials.

Abandoned to the adhesive floor tearing my quills from this skin.
Tethered to the reality of my chicks in my nest.
I must raise my fowl knowing how I was the reason Dad left.
I deprived these fledglings of a father's affection.

Forgiveness was never to fruition or I would soar the skies.
Resentment is what harbored me behind the walls of my cage and cries.
I wail ceaselessly as the virtual therapist promotes communication.
My shrill chirps sing of his affair to a woman recently divorced from her husband.

He claims his squawking was innocently only for emotional support.
He was her boss and his rouse fractured my trust at its core.
His office staff sent me violets with smiling cards sympathy,
Pitying my handicap as I remain caged on the floor in epiphany.

Every staff signature twisted my stomach,
Till I regurgitated the sympathy into the toilet.
Pleading for his redemption ark to earn back my trust.
He sat in a parking lot for hours exchanging texts with a slut.

Messages exchanged from his phone that were not professional.
She texts,"Te amo."
He swears on the lives of our children he is being only charitable.
He texts back,"Te quiero."

His claim of honesty drowned by lies and sneaking about town.
My beak gaped as my job performance fell into decline.
The thoughts of disappearing felt nice when I could no longer fly.
Flustered in the ceaseless "what if" ponderings of my shortcomings in life.
Sulking as I read his texts searching for a sign.
His bags remain packed by the front door tonight.
I text, "Te Amo".
He texts back, "Te Quiero".

EXIT
HARID WORKING
TRAVEL BACKS

Reminiscent

My present plight prevents me from paying,
I was put on medication from a doctor I can't afford.
I have major depression and generalized anxiety disorder.
Repetition of footsteps tracing the wood floor boards.

Walking halls like I am in a psych ward.
My husband's parents' home is not my own.
I am a burden with each creaking step forward,
I am not good enough like my Step-Dad screamed before,
Slamming cabinets till the hinges dislodge again from the split wood of the door.

She may ask me to fold the clothes waiting for the wardrobe.
Then I remember Step-Dad with an open palm to the back of my skull.
I would be thrown off balance and twist my ankles till I hit the floor null.

Creak.

His parents are so even tempered and royalty,
I relive in his parent's eyes every childhood mistake of mine.
They are not rude, but my anxiety will spike panic through my bones.
As the cortisol rages against my ever fluctuating hormones,
I prepare to be tripped by my Step-Father's boot's steel-toe.
I hit the ground.

Creak.

Shoved to the floor to pick up bread crumbs for mom.
Hit the ground.

Creak.

Pulled from my bed in my blankets and sheets.
Hit the ground.

Creak.

Forced to do push-ups till my arms broke beneath me.
Hit the ground.

Creak.

Patriarchal home with a narcissistic head.
A household that was created for floorboards to…

CREAK.

Now there is generosity and gracious energy upon me,
As I am provided shelter and financial stability.
Times were troubled and we were cast out,
Then his parents opened their door with empathy,
They welcomed us into their house.

But some days I cannot escape my mind and I hide,
Tucked away in my bed sheets as I listen quietly through the night,
For any trace footsteps down that lengthy hall.
Reliving the pain that forever haunts me as images flash from each fall.

Creak.

Unexpected

Shadows haunt each corner,
Piercing as they peer.
Noise distorted to static,
And a dull undertone of a saxophone is near.
Then they begin to start talking.
Reminiscent of Dante's Inferno,
Moaning, groaning, wailing,
Nonsensical blabbering to drown the pain and turmoil.

A cluster of commotion caught,
In the web of eternity,
A place where time holds no value.
The sounds clustered into a knot lacking security,
Leading the chorus under the bass tones,
Layering upon each other in my ear canal.
The intensity encompasses my cognition.
A consistent dictation of my insignificant fall,
And necessitates my demise by suicide,
An insufferable agony pushing delusional demise.
The racing speed of my heart spins faster than a top.
I am gutted, cleaned, and carved apart,
Laid out to dry as I shrivel and rot.

I quit my antidepressant three nights ago.
Flushed every pill from the child-proof bottle.
Flooded with instability I thought I would try to be normal.
Three years of wasted chemicals pressed from powder.
Without a taper I fear reality stemming from my black box label.

Now with incessant voices I have no pills to fix me.
All I desired was for the pill to not define me,
But my incursion for platitude only prospered a litany of agony.
This pain is lingering like a deep wound cursed with infectivity,
But sepsis would be a blessing next to this present suffering.

A curse creating regret with deep abysmal scarification.
Not a single scrap of hope to escape this relentless tyrannical invasion.

Feed Me

Financially stripped due to a new transmission.
I cannot render myself to live in such conditions.
Deprivation of necessities that feel so senseless,
Like the food we intake just to pass through our intestines.
Feels worthless to throw away money on nutrition,
But if I skip my lunch, it will make my friends anxious.
Their eyes will glare through my stomach lining.
This prying curiosity keeps my starvation out of hiding.
Hunger is so personal that their nosiness is violating.

If I could only abort myself from within the womb,
Of this life I have acquired eternally depleting.
To slide out stillborn on this miserable excursion,
Unable to engage in life's promised opportunities,
Deprived on those fundamental feelings,
That were taught and engrained within our psyche.
Casting a shadow of ourselves as some anomaly.
Inability to maintain a sense of financial security or career.
Walking a cycle of depravity that causes me to detest humanity.

I have gone on a hunger strike before to survive,
Those words drip with irony as they roll off the tongue without pride.
I will message you in five days so you know I'm still alive.
But I don't trust you to not imprison me, so I should say goodbye.
Resources are embarrassing to the image of the recipient,
I could never approach a food pantry with other invalids.
Nothing can save me but solely my own volition,
As I would rather go hungry and feel something,
Beyond this never ceasing pain that life affords me.

Left Behind

The frantic need to clean equated to be too much for me.
When I glance at the list of chores in my hands, it feels like infinity.
Suddenly the tasks accomplished fall short of any sense of glory.
It is a scratch on the surface of a century's worth of rust and decay.
The burnout feels inevitable and so the guilt begins to flood my veins.
Adjusting to the ever changing struggle to survive in a world of chaos and pain.

There is not spare second to take a break with the clutter I create,
Amongst a hoard of disappointing memories and utter fear of failing.
Relationships filled with toxicity that cause me to flee state lines.
Changing jobs and struggling to ensure a roof over my head at night.
It is this inevitable itch that can never be satisfied.

I moved for my partner.
Everything was new once again.
He cheated on me in November.
A constant tornado of physical altercations.
The depression kept me from breathing in.

Emotions are becoming numbed from incessant trauma compounding upon me.
I can no longer express my feelings and instead wander senselessly wasting time.
There is no organization amongst the deafening noise of this abandoned city.
To have a home where I am unknown and cry for something to occupy my mind.
My thoughts are repressed beyond sensibility,
Cradled in my fleeting dream’s depravity.

Worthless

My mother was a narcissist that greeted me with her fist.
Her faulty definitions of "love" left lingering shadows on my walls.
Years of abuse layered like snow where no Band-Aid will stick.
No contemplation left to whether I am to live, die, or be left alone.
The ashtray of her fags held more value than her own daughter.
Pressured to isolation in the spare bedroom's half bath.
Sitting next to the outlet under the glow of my phone.
Hoarding bottles of Mirtazapine to numb her accusatory tone,
As Mom let those who would defile me ask for dope at our home.

Her home became a crime scene to the subsequent underground.
Dealers stealing emotions for a baggie of white crystalline grounds.
I hide behind antipsychotics to stay a part of humanity.
Mom's eyes were already empty before she even chose a name for me.
I constantly linger on the periphery of a mental breakdown.
Detached myself from every falsified friend and my disenchanted family around.

Just tossed my pill bottles in the kitchen bin last Sunday.
Sissy peers around the corner with eyelashes batting my way.
I lay her back to bed cooing her with a fanciful fairy tale ending.
Being raised in the home of my Mother's shadows constant presence,
Places fear on a little girl's face that is only a young self-reflection.

I take fresh air to escape the claustrophobic sensations,
When every window turns to bars and a grim satisfaction.
Paramedics and police used to approach me like I'm crazy.
They are the ones that put the cuffs on my mother's wrists that day.
I am still judged like excrement due to the foulness of my mom,
That only bore me from a womb I had no choice in calling home.

And these psychosomatic seizures are labeled cries for attention.
It is funny how our saviors can turn their back with any distraction,
Worth more than the ash God himself used to form me.
The firefighters at Station 14 left me alone without my pills to support me,
So I numbed myself with alcohol and cried myself to sleep.
Tonight my eight year old lies next to me swaddled in her sheets.

I feel a bit better, I just need a different doctor to help me.

Lovesick

My kindred spirit and hearts companion,
Simply a facade behind my television screen.
She is as real as the Oxygen filling my lungs,
You may not see it but it's keeping me alive.
Ever-present in my life and my confidant.

Smothered by perpetual anxiety rendering me useless.
I have become a failure to my Supervisor and myself.
The residual stress and burnout created a Claymore mine.
A personal attack to my ego ending in resignation.
I even fail to take my own life due to residual trauma.

It was the fourth of July and my dad was off work all day.
It was almost time for fireworks as I dressed in red, white and blue.
My father wanted to play hide and seek and counted to ten.
I had to go find him.
A firework popped,
The show had begun.
Scurried down the halls while glancing out windows,
Hoping to see the light from the firecracker's ignite.
One more room left.
The Den.
Then I found him.
Sitting slumped behind the sofa.
I could only identify him by his house slippers and forearm tribal tattoos.
Twelve Gauge still in his arms.
Caressing it like one cradles a baby.
He was just so happy.
We were just playing.
I guess I won.

I could never kill myself.
The trauma taught me how to handle life's strife.
Not by punishing those around me by taking my life.
So I talked to my friend on the T. V. screen,
Or the posters on my wall where she gazes upon me.
I spill my pain and speak on my suicidal tendencies.
She knows just the right way to empathize and love me.
Started talking to her the day after the funeral service.
Millie was also far from perfect.
She was abused and traumatized.

She became my key to stay alive.

Hours of ceaseless word salad from scrambled thoughts in a shattered skull.
She never judges me and always forgives me for that unwanted victory.
She gave me breath when I am depleted and kept me far past expiration.
No one understands my fascination,
With the unbiased nature of a fictional character.
Unlike the audacious world around me,
With it hypocrisy and morbid mockery in jest.
Millie is always reliable and eternally with me.
She will incessantly care about me.
Sound in her convictions and is no adjudicator,
Only an undying best friend.
Eternal Salvation behind an LCD screen,
Or perfectly printed on glossy parchment.
Forever coddling me with her eye's embrace.

Spiraling Down

Long-distance love,
He becomes irate when I am upset.
I crave his voice to send me to slumber.
He calls me asinine at the request.
His focus has shifted from me,
As he chooses to meditate to music in solidarity.
I am sensitive.
Mortified by my intrusive insecurities,
Irrational propositions of anxious thinking.
"He never desired me form the start."
My newfound tears now spark his hostility.
Heartlessly he screams before virtually disconnecting.
Electricity pummels into my chest cavity.
Proceed to steal a blade from a razor used for shaving.
Praying cuts on my leg will relieve my weeping.

Suddenly a notification illuminates a text,
It displays a simple message of "K.Y.S." from my ex.
Flashes blind me of him pinching my upper arm or thigh,
Then wagging his finger stressing that I starve myself or die.
He would hang a cloud of inevitable heart disease,
When I gained five pounds last spring.
I was reminded how lucky I was he didn't leave me.
No one would want a lard laden monstrosity.
I started dragging my fingers down my throat,
As his laughter echoed outside the bathroom door.
If I threatened to leave his tyranny would arise.
He layered passive threats of harm,
Spoke of sending others to ensure my demise.
Even burning down my family home with everyone inside.
I desperately sought an order of restraint,
After calls of threats from VoIP numbers refused to refrain.
The police only stated to block the contact and wait.
The perfect storm cocktail at expert time.
Some omnipresent force's plan has aligned,
All in an effort to cause me pain and duress tonight.

A call interrupted my stumbling train of thoughts,
It was an apologetic boyfriend with a lackluster response,
Carrying guilt for hurting me yet again.
But words never cure the trauma inflicted.

And then the nauseating thoughts start flooding in.
The flashbacks create a pondering cry,
“What would it be like if I was not alive?”
Then I tumble down the rabbit hole,
Childhood rape for drugs exchanged ages ago,
Then ripped away far too late by a DFCS staff.
Placed in foster care under a new address.
This triggers the feelings of my Ex violating me,
Then thoughts of how friends only ever use me.
I simply continue to allow the abuse to layer upon me.

All I desire is acceptance and contentment.
Love is an illusion, but I’ll take a genuine friend,
To hold a sense of purpose in the debauchery of mortality.
Or just to help distract me from life’s daily inferno of a reality.
Instead, the sensation of insignificance still reigns.
Imagining if my death would leave an impact on the world remaining.

USED 4 MONEY
USED 4 MONEY
YOUR FAT
ABANDONED
NO FRIENDS
KMS
PARENTS
HURT U
KMS
SUCK UP

Happy You

"Birthday" echoes around the corner like a ticking bomb,
A sour note reverberating mortality on the taste buds of mankind.
Ring tones roll out relatives inquiring on my gaieties.
Dead air rests heavy on the phone line as my mind struggles to fib.
I crack under the cumbersome weight as I search words to express,
The normalcy of this day without feeling unmerited.
Yielded under the ineffable shade to secure myself in the dark.
I mope with repressed fury over the childhood stolen from me.

A child's voice muffled till fully silenced by a lashing,
Soon taught that words were best lost in the void ever lingering,
A drift in the air with shared breaths of thoughts inhibited.
Lost words saltier than the Pacific Ocean marooned on my taste buds,
Yielding my lips to crack till spit and bleeding from dehydration.
Too parched to speak a word that didn't yield a painful whisper.

Living this eternal internal mummification,
Where a detached clot creating a terminal embolism,
Is more of a godsend than continuing this day of reminiscing.
My husband appears flabbergasted by my audacious act,
Failing to see into the pit of trauma Dad had gifted me.
No amount of words could be sensible enough to depict,
The beatings received from piercing strikes of his switch.

My thoughts began to melt like a warm gelatinous dessert.
Tears heated by anger at the core of a broken childhood.
The day ended with a simple hug and "good night, dear".
Left in the silhouette of my trauma while wide awake in this nightmare.
Eyes open, lying in bed with racing thoughts of childhood memories,
Dancing the Waltz with the shadows aggressively looming over me.
Even still, I predicate, this was far from my worst birthday.

Lullaby

Incessant ticking never stops,
I cannot escape the thunderous clock.
It reminds me of the snare which I am stuck,
Unable to find comfort in abstract thoughts.
Dreams zipping through my mind in a daze,
With the blaring white light behind my eyes forming a haze.
No matter how drained of energy,
Each atom of my body aches to be free.
My brain cannot stop screeching.
The discomfort in my extremities,
Relentless tossing and turning,
Turning and tossing,
To no satisfaction or avail emerging.
My tissue paper sanity navigates me,
As I complete day five of my electrified mind.
Fighting any need to close my eyes,
Wires twisted and frayed,
Batteries becoming corroded in time.
My cerebrum is begging to fry,
Sitting on the edge of short-circuiting,
With no relief in sight.
Plummeting hopelessly with pills,
Trazodone, Seroquel, Gabapentin,
Remeron, Atarax, Doxepin.
Prescription labeled Antipsychotics,
Antidepressants, and Blood Pressure Medications.
All used off label with a litany of side effects,
To fail to fix my lack of rest.
Mother once gave me her Ambien,
I actually had a decent slumber again.
Doctors fear patients will become addicted.
Truthfully I can guarantee a death from O.D.,
With the off-label poisons prescribed to me.
Useless pills rattling in my mind,
Encouraging an answer of permanent sedation and decline.
Avoiding school that is hanging on by a scholarship.
Thoughts twisted and snapped like crushed twigs,
To the point I think about stealing Mom's Ambien.
But I cannot hurt her just because of a doctor's fearfulness,
So the thoughts of the pharmacy in my cabinet lingers, hence,
I cannot suffice a sixth night on this last thread of competence.

Nervous

I wet my jammies and my bed sheet.
Normally my diaper absorbs it.
I do not want to wake up Mommy.
She may be grumpy because she is tired.
How long would it take for them to dry?
Both the sheet and the jammies?
I do not want to bother Mommy.
I do not know if she will be angry.
My diaper has always absorbed it.
This is the first time I am not dry.
Can you tell me how to clean everything?
I do not want to have to wake Mommy up.
Do you have any Children?
Do you know if it will dry or not for sure?
What do I tell my Mommy when I wake her?
Please wait while I go wake Mommy.
I want to tell you how good I did after.
I am back and Mommy changed everything.
She did it so fast, she was not mad at all.
It was so fast that I forgot to tell her,
I have to go potty again now.
And I already have my new diaper on.
I can't change my diaper on my own.
Do you think my diaper will keep me dry?
I do not want to bother Mommy again.
I am gonna try to potty and see what happens.
It kept me dry, so I can now go to bed.
Thank you for being so kind to listen to me.
Goodnight.

Spectrum

We are both on the spectrum,
Communicating without veracity.
My tone can come across varied.
There is not a clear cut way to interpret,
When my head can't register how I sound.

My tone's perception by others is faltering.
He made the false assumption I wanted isolation.
I am the introverted socially stunted girl stereotype,
But truly there were tormenting emotions enamoring me.
An utter melancholy riddled through my chromosomes.
Radiating alarms of distress he was blind to.
Any cue he inferred that I needed seclusion baffles me.
He quickly turned his back to go gallivanting with mates.

I am stuck in this murky marsh glued to the sticky mud.
My feet sunk into its grip pulling me down with the reeds.
Left to a ruminant evening of thoughts imprisoning me.
Suicide laid on a platter as a key to escape my body's dredging.
If he only sensed the uncertainty of my emotional decline,
I would not hold these thoughts of depravity so tight around my neck.

Each time he is unwell I cater to his wounds and coddle him.
To give all my energy to simply see his pain be alleviated.
Yet, here I am stranded in the grime consumed by dense fog.
The marsh is slowly devouring me in this epitome of misery.
Covered by the infinite herbaceous life like a funeral spray.
I can hear the plants breathe intrepidly while I suffocate.
The water fills my lungs as I realize I have brought this on myself.

Home

Give me the grace of knowing your face one last time.
Give me the grace of hearing your voice fade into the night.

Grace.

I never wanted to leave Massachusetts.
The way your bows were tied at the bottom of your braids,
The headband pulling back the fine hairs,
Like taut wires feeding into the circuitry of your brain.
The tiniest freckles lining the bridge of your nose.
A window to a world of compassion unknown.

Grace.

I am only an apparition and you are only a memory.
You never knew what became of me, I simply vanished against proclivity.
If this paper was worth a damn, it would bring you back to me.
But this letter is only a fallen petal of a life you long wrote off.

Grace,

Since leaving, the shelter has been my only home.
Evictions piled upon my mother leaving me to work to the bone.
My GED brought toxic work environments at retail stores.
Mother showcases no empathy, just cigarette burns.

Grace.

The masquerade masks of glitter and feathers,
Decorated for Mardigras week at middle school.
She was enamored with the Red, black and gold,
Glittering across a row of crow feathers I had created.

Grace.

She will touch the dried spit I place on this adhesive,
As she opens to find my list of contrite words in shattered pieces.
But the cynical person within me begs I just push her away,
Powerless to the vindictive world that spirals around me each day.

Grace.

Over a decade and I cannot escape your grasp on me.
The mirror in the motel bathroom reminds me of my inhospitality.
My reflection has already cracked the glass encapsulating me.

Craving a shard to grip in my hand to only be cut prematurely.

Grace,

Memories are such a cruelty as it traps our mind in a bubble of time.
If I went back home to you, you are just a husk of the person I knew.
Shed and undefined by the past that I eternalized like a diamond in a coal mine.
You would be independent and grown, angel in transfiguration and blue.

Grace.

It is the thought of her that burrows weaving tunnels in my mind,
That dug up various images of the childhood I had once surmised,
Pushing them into the forefront of my mind's eye till a migraine shall arise,
Consuming me in a pulsating rhythm in sync with my heart time.
I imagine my heartbeat aligns with hers,
Screaming "I just want to go home and call you 'mine'".

Isolate

Fixate and postulate, but never more than once.
A bee traversing to the nectar and back to the honeycomb,
Provides efficiency and is on a one-track mindset.
My one-track mind does not come with common sense.
I harbor no sense of rationality and will forgo what's important.

Rearranging the herbaceous potted recluses to catch a glimpse of the best rays.
Overlook grocery necessities or rotating and assorting the laundry of the day.
Lack of daily significance yields missed medical appointments.
My mind's eye always fleeting to only fixate on one unnecessary anxiety.
Days emerge of sedimentary privacy with exception to racing ponderings.
They compile and compound into accumulated resurfacing traumatic reminiscing.

I found myself on the steps to my parental home with wife in tote.
Mom's new partner only a boy still living with parents and lacking income to float.
Her fling has a passion for video games and his parent's financials for reaping.
He craves to parent me aggressively, when the misfortune is our paths crossing.

Mom solely hollers indifference to my feelings,
Favoring her honeymoon engagement as he now leeches off her purse strings.
He moved into a sanctified home to simply ransack the abode.
My mother works two jobs to keep both their bills afloat.
Disrespect dished and served on audacious tonality of gracious mentality.
Soon whispers spoiled the adulatory with his exposure to adulterous reality.
Mom's a fractured marionette pulled by his egotistical strings,
As she ties his boot laces in the morning with no bickering.

Migraine beetles dig rampant holes to escape my temples in holiday nightmares,
Their burrowing only spreads the headache of consequential disease and fears.
Soon the fluttering and twitching of their wings beat against my skullcap in wallow.
Nauseousness soon is presenting with just a glance at his wide-set furrowed brow.
Barely "home".
Soon the overstimulation sends my brain to shut down.
Earbuds replace his puffed out lungs as all is drowned out in musical sound.
I take my venture to the deepest open patch of land encircled by brush,
To holistically drift into the company of birds and squirrels exploring nooks.
My meditative state sends me into doze without a single needle prick.
Left a feast of bread crumbs like Christmas Eve,
Knowing upon my reawakening was their impending absence.

A cold creek ripples white noise melodies beyond the music to send me adrift.
Till my wife comes to encourage me awake,
My wife left behind to explain reason for my absence from the day.
The reality was that I did not belong there at this age,
I was simply part of their disembodied consensus and atypical flair,
Chronically subjugated o the disillusioned state of their holiday fanfare.

Confidence

Social media brought us together by chance.
The intersecting web entwined,
Producing an incantation generating his face in happenstance.
Insecurity crawling across each cell of my epidermis.
I blackened out my lens to calm the rebellion in my veins procuring.

Mom taught me to remember the shame of my dark skin.
These Arabian genetics were conquered by the East African.
Blood running thicker from the side of a father unknown.
Only gifted daily reminders through the flaws of skin tone.

I was the black spot left behind by Davy Jones.
Such an anxious interlude till the Kraken consumes me whole.

Computer screens provide armor to shield my flawed complexion.
His struggle with discrimination ignited empathy instilling my investment.
We became tethered through shared interests from music to life goals.
Hours passed in flashing moments so quick imprinting upon my soul.

Then an utterance snared me as he was racist towards my veneer.

To allow a glance of my face could constitute liberation.
The walls that have encompassed me becoming fractured at the foundation.
Crumbling its brittle sediment to breathe a sense of integrity.
Like diving into freezing waters and feeling the sting dissipate me,
Then finding myself floating on the water's surface beaten by rays.
Igniting a sense of security through my once compromised body.

The concept of such a bond to be so fleeting from the shade of my ancestry,
Was not to drag me down to drown as I will emerge from the waters dripping,
Shedding the insecurities to confidently own my identity,
As the weight of the world runs off my body lifting prior shame indefinitely.
And though there is a screen between us I will be seen,
As I leave my insecurities to drown at sea.

UGLY
UUGLY
WORTHLESS
LOUY
TERRILESS
EGOILE
LOATHE

Truth Hurts

Flashing lights beat against my corneas,
As a "G" chord reverberates against my ear drum.
The pick extended off his thumb morphing man with instrument.
The blur of reality smeared with the titration of a drum solo.
A single thump of a bass turned into a stampeded of resonance unwavering.
Humanoid figures crammed like scurrying rats in a mosh pit enclosure.
Soon only primitive shrieks and squeals were all encompassing.

Electricity spikes fire through each brain cell in a radiant branching of chaos.
Perpetual stimulation poured through systematic travel down my nervous system.
My body ignites in pure lightning strikes at my raw nerve endings.
Engulfing any sensibility as my stomach was contorted unnaturally.

I grab the faux leather sleeve of my fiancé's illusively deceiving supportive nature.
Inability to express an utterance of my excruciating agony of immediate existence.
He places the car keys my rabbit paw shaking and fawning for empathy.
I ran out of luck as his breath of contempt wafted over me,
The primal craving to escape for self-preservation left me to flee the vicinity.

Arriving at the car I can feel my breath succumb to the sense of strangulation,
From the invisible grip of the external chaotic stimuli against the nape of my throat.
Collapsing into my car seat a wave of burden and shame bite into my neck.
My gut is swallowed by the self-loathing of my decisive abandonment,
Layered with the illusion of residual tactile stimulation from a faux leather coat.

Remembering the donations that sustained me as I was kept captive,
Held in a group home harbored by predators of the state from my own parents.
Craving the abuse and neglect from my own biology over mandated reports.
Slipping into the background static where no one asked if I was suicidal.

There never was a signal.

I am the utter annoyance that always seems to linger above tempo.
Praying one day I can rest beyond this imploding crescendo of cadence.

Shade

Burnt out.

I am: Student, Employee, and Mother.
I daydream of my own annihilation.
Some outside force to intervene,
Stealing me away from the depravity,
Of the prospect of an unfathomable future.

Burnt out.

A small ant lugging an enormous leaf in the sun's rays,
Beaten in the heat under the burdensome foliate crushing his legs.
Unable to bring shame to his colony,
Left to venture endlessly on a winding pheromone journey,
Till the bends of his knees give way.
"Snap and crack," scream his contorted extremities!
The pest drags along his mangled body.
The shade of a corpse shielding from the sun's beams,
Ultimately recoiling under the leaf that facilitated destruction.
Left with a lack of salvation there is only consummation.

Burnt out.

Haunted by the specter of my son's still autumn birth.
Stripped of the embodiment of motherhood.
Derealization permeates all reality.
Slipping into dissociated daydreams.
Craving an escape button.
Surrealism lingering in perpetual motion.
Bathing in the echo of post mortem humanity.
Weaving through the shadows of my procreation.
Lamenting the lack of purpose with each breath.
Left to fault my son for this strife,
Or accept this predisposition to crumble and fragment.

Burnt out.

Swelling with the sand in the belly of a whale.
Debris is far from welcoming.
Attempting to dig out of its gullet or become regurgitated.
Begging to be washed onto shore.
Greeted by an ant eager to share some shade,
Unwilling to die alone.

Mama

Her lingering curse she just can't shake.
Each outstretched arm swatted from embrace.
Father molded words to only highlight his favor.
Mom's pills in the waste basket of life's proclivities.
His smirk tied knots in Mom's laces and bows of layers.

My nursery's pink bonnet set fire to my father's insecurities.
Mom quivered in the lingering silhouette of his vexation.
Father fled to reproduce an off springs of King's royalty.
Mom fancied dreams of pushing my stroller into traffic.
Father became enamored with the son of a fertile Queen,
As Mom would rather choke down mucus than show affection to me.

Resentment was more familiar than love in our home.
Father's rum on my gums could not numb my cries.
His affairs seeded trails beyond what numbers quantify.
A lineage threaded through naivety as I wept alone.
An infantile complication to my Mom's beauty regimen.
Her dying vitality was Father's "not guilty" plea against accusations of sin.

An utterance echoed through the raven's calls,
Fumbling through shadows towards the route of "Nevermore".
Sulking in the dense air pinned between vacant bedroom walls,
Harboring reminiscent glimpses flashing confinement and fear.
Pressed against the gravel of my own life's determination.
The unraveling of my life reveal permanent knots of rumination.

Upon the dawn of emergence,
I finally concluded this path I furrowed,
Falling six feet beneath a freshly unearthed burrow.
The moon spits shards of light over a ravenous grave.
Greeted by Mom's gaze.
Looming with the volatility of her pickaxe.
Placing the judgement of God upon me as she stole my name back.
Spitting on identity with narcissism and an animosity facade.
Left abandoned to relive every mistake I was told I made.

Failure

There is no comfort in oxygenated lungs.
Licensed to carry and an expert with a shotgun.
I restlessly begged to take the rest of the pill bottle.
Failure yields regret that I had not died in my teenage waddle.
Decades of a brain simply wired differently.
No triggers or traumas excusing my finality.
As my paranoia spikes my own wife's anxiety,
I have birthed a relationship entwined with toxicity.
My burden damages the only grace God gave me.
I have driven away male friends with delusions that sway me,
Formulated by the personal insecurities kept.
Drinking to nullify the memories imprints. .
Regrets not sewn but branded into the fabric of eternity.
Unmistakable and irreplaceable in the light of elation and rationality. .
The epiphany that I am better dead than sanctification.
No mixture of prescriptions can curb my insanity's pervasion.
Forever lost in the back alley of the pub that knows my gait precisely.
Teasing the leader of the ordinary proclivity that is made about me.
Truthfully, it is the only reality that my neuronal paths can muster anyway.
My drinking leaves nothing but empty threats and diffidence in my way.
I had no desire to cause these cracks in her foundation to split.
Yet the scars I laid upon her are far from being caulked with sealant.
And if the trimmer of my steps could echo any sense of truth known,
I would be a ghost to you so your blood could finally clot,
And you could finally feel whole as I fade amongst the lot.

Rope

A million of fragile fibers,
Woven into a strong bind.
Pull them apart,
Their strength is illusive,
Much like the finite fibers of my mind.
Torn apart,
They hold no weight.
Singular and finite.

I have no ground to stand on.
If I could only be as strong,
As the rope that tethers my throat,
To this aluminum closet rod.

Wealth has no meaning,
When the words fall from delphinium lips.
And the branches I bear are sturdy,
But the leaves wither from false glory.
I am left barren with stripped bark,
Seeking redemption from wood rot.
Placid in my story arc.

This game of diluted delusion,
Recollecting the false idol erected,
Of Paper saturated in ink,
Where the right number can steal anyone's morals reflections,
Defined by green dye and hypocrisy's conceptions.

An innocent dance of cat and mouse.
Truly I am cleansed of this futile ruse,
With comfort found in the harmonious bind,
Eager to expire on my God allotted time,
Destined to yield no fruition in strife.
Letting go into a disassociated bodily tithe,
To satisfy the liquidation of senseless life.
To fulfill the lucrative cycle for God's chosen,
Eradicating the unnecessary human rife.

Overseas

Epitome of isolation in a foreign land.
Captured in the web woven by endearments.
Lured by my broken sense of attachment.
Desiring to be another's obsession.
Left with two permanent marks to my self-perception.

Partners lashing out, defining my insecurities.
Falling victim as I take no accountability.
Waste so vile and toxic, encasing me in a heavy sludge,
Weighing me down and putting me in my place.
Left to my own putrefaction from endless betrayal.
Escaping both circular trauma narratives inlayed,
To redefine myself with appeared to be a genuine face.

Then one day his wife and children walked into our place.

With each and every prospect comes a demand,
Sexual exchange for monetary gain.
Conceptually adding pressure to the years of bruising,
Flashes of popped buttons and torn seams ensuing,
The stain of beer across my blouse nauseates me.
As he pulls my locks to force me to his position of pleasure.
His ego a blur and the last breath stripped from me in my underwear.

Psych Wards greeted me with lengthy holidays.
Labels dripping off my collar bone like PTSD, BPD, and MDD.
Pellets shot into my genome unleashing chemical trails.
Neurons spark till capsized in a bog of deceased transmission.
Potions attempt to regulate a decrepit sympathetic nervous system.

This sinking ship once promised me rejuvenation,
Now I crave my mother's arms to embrace me in acceptance.
Let her Whisper to me through the sticky salted air,
As I take my last breath before I am submerged in the Atlantic.

Overdose

I dommwjana die.
I just hury so bad.
Im so terihbke.
O fele sock.
I cain Frekly stand
Yowu knw my birthday was twll days ago.
Isntop taking medidcation caushd it sucks.
Indont like seeing a thehrpaist.
I feel sonheorrible.
Ive goofbe so fat and I deel so torrible.
Shodul I tell whr?
She say I scarexherr.
My fienwd didny even caer.
Mus bestidirienddhatesss meeew.
I cany, I cajt.
I don wna her to be mad.
She alrjeisd alwusd so amd at ke.
I should go theb shospiyal again.
If I dgo to sleep wil k die?
I nenefhlep.
Imsoru.
Mu head heiysbso bad.
It hirts so muc.
Evjethingbhurts.
My gehead is poudnib.
But i jsu want to be lcoef.
The giy I loevd left meee.
Why dod seveuon ehatevme?
An devfrione thinks in stuoud.
I dorn have self-repxknd.
I ryin my own biruhday and eveyijne hate me. .
Ibejydt wanna be oskay.

DOCTORS

Daddy's Home

Transitioned to be the father I never had.
Met with an ex who kept me in the position of homelessness.
Sleeping in my car to the sound of radio static,
With a broken antenna and lack of patience.
Bartering for a few nights at a motel to shower,
Money is only fleeting as I dream of bringing my son home.

I hold no home in my heart.
So I resort to tinged crystals in a clouded pipe.
Rolling the cylindrical salvation in my fingers,
Praying it won't burn as the illicit wisp of smoke promises life.
Smoke slithering through the nodules in my lungs,
Opening up my chest to elude a pair of wings.
Irrevocably blessed with transient breath,
An illusion of being free.

Borderline between emotional extremes,
Attempted seven times with no luck of relief.
Three years of a deity pushing me back to Earth.
Eternal numbing of this emotional intensity,
Striving to remain where I have found my comfort,
With the baggie in my pocket as I fumble my lighter.

I once was grounded by the grip pads on insanity's feet.
6:00 A.M. wake-up calls to ensure my heart was beating.
Pills popped in rainbow colors in this dispensary.
Tissue thin gowns and cups made from paper carelessly.
Bending pens of rubber, made so they can't hurt me.

Everything is a cycle.

Released without a parasol to keep my biodegradable fit dry.
Simply a paper bag left on a street corner calling to the roaches and rats awry,
Discovering freedom under a damp piece of cardboard.
I Consumed Benzos and Methamphetamine,
The pavement became a cloudy throne of power.
All washed down by a shot of whiskey as my riptide crashed amongst the rocks.

Faulty residue of burnt char creates thin flakes of ash to be flicked off the glass. .
Another bowl tarnished by the wavering hand stifling the rise of my smoke
Transparent premature shards barricading me from the vaporous spirit untethered,
The World's afflictions entice the spirit as I cry for my son to come home.

Hopeless

I have taken all your medications.
I have gone to each therapy session.
I have been inpatient nine times.
I have challenged every negative thought.
I have said every positive affirmation.
I have gone on daily walks.
I have used grounding techniques when dissociated or anxious.
I have written in my journal each morning and night.
I have prioritized focusing on my physical health.
I have volunteered to help others and share wealth.
I have attended each group therapy meeting.
I have created five different vision boards.
I have filled 33 composition books with writing.
I have completed EMDR treatment.
I have meditated every afternoon and evening.
I have created the habit of deep breathing.
I have adjusted my day and night to a healthy routine.
I have integrated coping skills into my daily schedule.
I have recited my list of gratitude before bedtime.
I have taken all the vitamins my body needs to thrive.
I have gone to every scheduled doctor's screening.
I have had regular bloodwork four times a year.
I have cut carbs and sugars out of my diet entirely.
I have adopted an emotional support dog named Theo.
I have replaced self-harm with Henna tattoos.
Yet I still look at my bottle of antidepressants that numb me,
And desire to take every last one and pray to never wake up.

YOUR
I AM
WORTHY
IAMM
I AM
LOVED
LOVED
Sertraaline

Overloaded

Ninety hours.

Nonstop work to scrape a buck for a roof.
Delineating between burnout, homelessness, or death.

Ninety hours.

Thoughts dissolve into a hazy cloud of distorted fragmentations.
Apprehension of the ticking clock while perverting the hours past.

Ninety hours.

The gravel scrapes my knees as I fawn at my vulnerable raw flesh.
Praying the blood from the abrasion will be enough to atone me.

Ninety hours.

Clawing through a cesspool of addiction to finally reveal an air pocket,
Unraveling my epiphany that life has no relief as I teeter on its periphery.

Ninety hours.

Familial bound by blood steadfast to disown me as I remain in recovery.
They favor another nail in my coffin and propose another foot of depth to my grave.

Ninety hours.

Uncovering only castaway relationships with a sexual transaction on the first date,
Triggering tormented images of the men who assaulted me in my dope haze.

Ninety hours.

Swallowed in my comforter ruminating on my last attempt with sleeping pills,
Stricken to a fifteen percent survival rate only to recover with a new plan of intent.

Ninety hours.

Precariously vetting any open store for the OTC sleeping pills to suffice,
Abandoned in a derelict waste of a town with no means to end my suffering tonight.

Ninety hours.

I am only allotted four hours of sleep before my next sixteen hours of shift work.
The blood drips down my calves as onlookers stare, but no one says a word...

Fly Away

Even when you waned I still would go my way.
The neglect became a habitual mistake.
My serpent tongue articulated every word you desired.
Ultimately your eyes glazed as I still inflicted pain.
I diluted your reality to the taste that suited my cravings.
The clouded staircase winded a path with no apparent culmination.
You had lost your glass slippers miles prior,
But no one had come knocking at your door with inclination.

Your irises flourished spitting back light like crystals,
Vexed, as our son suckled, nuzzled to your breast.
He was the gem that ignited your adoration.
My synthetic fervor spoiled by an infant's clasp.

With my ruse unraveling infinite resentment,
I fostered change through therapeutic intervention.
Incessantly polishing what will always be an imitation.
Failing to satisfy you with my display of self-deprecation.
Hopelessly feigning a metamorphosis for your satiation.

You choose to depart across bodies of water to evade me.
Our helpless son is torn from the crumb of empathy I honed,
Leaving me to expel this oil slick from my lungs,
As I thrash in the waters gasping for you to come home.

Draining

To loathe the Industrial Revolution,
Implanting a seed of a lucrative magnate.
Too young to be so emboldened with efficiency.
Maturity was subjugated by the ego I portrayed.
A lost juvenile amongst influential prospectors,
Salivating at the thought of puppeteering just a boy.
Ignorance begot regrets as the tailspin spiraled.
The fruit of life lost the chance to ripen to the bruises I abode.
Opportunities chewed holes through the bitter rind,
Eating the flesh of my potential and leaving me to rot behind.
I squandered deals with a lack of social skills while acting nervy,
Navigating me to trust the guidance of these hungry larvae.
Chewed through my ambition to its core,
I finally faltered enough to see the butterflies soar.
Left to decompose in the shade of their wings,
Pondering if a seed will sprout once again.
I now push my nose into the pages of aged textbooks.
Faulty isolation comforted by the words in intellectual nooks.
Hollow knowledge replayed as I remained confined in solitary.
Picking up fictional tales in hopes of transposing mind to imaginary.
Adapting characters' lives where dreams are still alive.
Yet the fractured yearning for aspiration still stalks me inside.
Aimless in a purgatory of rejection and cracked glass.
Passing patrons in observation of my work in the judge of class.
Reflecting on each art piece in the glow of a dying ember.
Blissfully ignorant to the boy who gave it the wings to fly forever.
Admiring the second-hand regurgitation of a childhood dream.
Piecing together fragmentations of broken shards of me.
Smiling at a mirror image,
Of what I once crafted from the trenches,
Leaving only one lingering thought in my dystopian mind,
"Why is God's hate towards me so inclined?"

Catching Flight

Words only inadequately alieve my situation.
My problems are for my private self-consultation.
Therapeutic inquires plaster cement bricks about my frame.
All the inquiries in therapy builds walls around me.
Further isolating me in this insufferable medical game.
Though advice is not a vice but a welcomed remedy,
Specificity is not a necessity when begetting friendly.
Yet, mankind is purely deplorable and infuriating.
Draining my respite through the fight to assert against these adversaries.
Ultimately rejected through their belittling breath,
Boundaries service priceless measures to only be disrespected.
Left to putrefy in my own sense of isolation.
The harmonies and melodies perpetuated,
Through my thick foam headset consoling me.
The bass heaves, radiating through my extremities,
Canceling the noise of ignorance's suffocating visit,
Enveloped in bars composed of staffs of silk and velvet.
Wrapped in its cocoon to seek personal maturation.
Reminded of my own integrity as I grapple fruition,
To persevere through other's slander with this transmutation.
I can then put behind me the ostracization,
As I flutter high above the ostentatious egos,
Proclaiming the definitive path that is my own.

The Cycle

Stuffed into a black Sedan, his head peeked over his shoulder,
Tear ducks swelled as the car door slammed signaling it was over.
Transported with a garbage back of chipped toys and soiled clothes.
Forsaken alone with this decrepit trailer where grief stole my home.

Shame stripped me bare with a beer in hand,
Silencing the incessant wailing imprinted.
Dulling the flashes of pumping her chest for air,
Fading the false hope once harbored as ribs were fractured.
Each compression she adamantly dissipated in my essence.
My daughter's eyes fell still as the dispatcher mumbled in silence.

My skin prunes in my toxic submersion into this numbing amber.
Numbingly nauseated in a haze of neglect upon my only son procreated.
Mourning a daughter damned by the opiates my mother harbored,
Gifted to a husband whose responsibilities wasted in his drug induced slumber.
Left with life's prism that refracts the light in a dozen directions,
Showcasing the possibilities of the paths in life untaken.

Slathered with programs and recovery reformation,
Caricatures of humanity tickling conceptualizations of sober indoctrination.
Propositioning the process to be elemental in execution,
When grief's thick sticky syrup has encapsulated my heart's entire function.

I fumble for pills to mix with half a pint of whisky dry,
To float away in the gentle sway of the rolling tide.
Picturing my daughter with her vacant eyes falling into mine,
Imagining my son questioning "why" as I float away from seaside.

Ground

Existing in the disfigured contortion of my mind's eye.
Obscured gaze placed upon this theatrical scene of life persisting.
Contemplating the narrative arcs of the characters surrounding.
Absorbed in the distilled silence of the world confounding me.
Observing the purpose filled entities floating in my gravitational field.
Displaced from the performance as I feel dazed in other's distorted yield.
A stray balloon with weak skin lost in the absentminded wind.
Craving a needle to pop this poison so I can finally descend,
Only to blunder and miss the rubber,
Puncturing my feeble heart in blunder.
Unable to deflate and tumble back into the shell of my body.
Losing sight of any permanence in the act remaining floating.
Wondering when the curtain will come to a close.
On this long awaited final show.

Am I Worthy?

Far wiser than the ignorance used to excuse their behaviors.
My parents' cannot undue the wickedness I grew into.
An eternal cycle of replicating the abusive arm of trauma predicating.
I shoved my supports deep in the hole I dug for myself to stew.
Shepherded to the far back corner to be stripped of my armor.
Awaiting the abuse that cannot be evaded as I cradle our newborn.
The umbilical cord is a tether to the man I need to flee.
Or possibly an excuse to let me ride the Ferris wheel till morn.
And as the clouds waft over our heads I no longer can see the ground.
I feel a surge of shock shoot through my marrow and down my spine.
The steel swing rattled from the energy that was generated.
I turn and no longer can make out the face of the man sitting at my side.
Then I whisper to the daughter clutched in my arms, "I won't let go".
Knowing if we were to drop my body would cushion her fall through embrace.
With each hit I take I am reminded of the guilt and shame.
When the clouds dissipate he then caresses the bruises on my face.
I can relieve my lungs and am assured the chaos has receded.
Ashamed to match her gaze with every yell, slam, and slap engrained.
I am predisposing my daughter to be a victim of the slaughter.
The pain will never truly die out in this relentless cycle we call home in shame.

Locked Away

Cracks weave instability through the concrete beneath my feet.
The burnt sienna stains on the copy paper sheets gnashes against my anxiety.
Never fathomed a key could hold such gravity till it governed my existence.
Practicing placing my hands in prayer to mimic the glimpse of a passing tattoo.
Pondering the process of mixing ash for ink and the pain behind each prick.
I try to focus on a prayer I was worthy to have pass my lips.
Envisioning my wife behind these same bars serving a dime for a mistake.
Guards cackle as they rap their baton against steel during rounds between breaks.
At night the incandescent bulb in their torch is mistaken for a cherubim.
Counting the sways of her cradle in the fleeting thoughts before slumbering.
Pondering if I cross my wife's mind amongst the criminal decay.
On bond fluttering through hate mail while mulling in a job terminality.
Crumbling death threats like casted stones holding no accountability.
Triggered by the incessant smell of Mom's loitering half-drunk wine glasses.
One night of inebriation became the thief of two passing pedestrians.
Haunted by the singular word painting crimson lines across asphalt.
Lost in the purgatory of an impending hearing as my daughter cries.
Ignorant of her mother and what procured from a double vehicular homicide.

ABOUT THE AUTHOR

Kyleen Elizabeth Oldham holds a Master's degree in Trauma and Crisis Care from Liberty University and has worked with a vast variety of individuals as counselor and psychiatric technician. She has been involved with those in foster care, worked with geriatric clients, assisted with those who had intellectual and developmental disabilities, as well as addicts in recovery. Her passion is working with youth and providing the care, empathy, resources, and support to assist in managing their mental health while still young to have the hope for the best future ahead. Kyleen has been working with clients in crisis in person and via a crisis hotline and has done so for many years. She has always had a passion for creative writing and hopes the poetic energy behind the words with the imagery she has created can covey a glimpse into the community she serves through her work. She hopes that it may not only bring out empathy from those who read, but also allow readers to realize that we are all human and as such we should be there for one another. No one deserves to feel alone.

Made in the USA
Columbia, SC
07 January 2025

49736112R00122